C A P R I

From the Stone Age to the Tourist Age

by

Arvid Andrén
Sometime Director of the Swedish Institute
of Classical Studies in Rome

1 9 8 0
Paul Åströms förlag
Göteborg

CONTENTS

© Arvid Andrén 1980
Printed in Italy
ISBN 91 85058 98 X
Agnesotti, Viterbo 1980

PREFACE

Capri has probably seen more dramatic events and more extraordinary people on its own soil and in the vicinity than any other small island in the world. Its rocks have been trodden by palaeolithic and neolithic troglodytes, by Greeks and Romans, by Lombards and Normans, Saracens and Turks, Italians, Frenchmen, Spaniards, Englishmen, and in our day, by people from all over the world. Its history presents a colourful gallery of distinctive characters: Emperor Augustus and Emperor Tiberius, the depraved Gaius Caligula, the adventurous Herod Agrippa, later king of the Jews, St. Constantius, the beautiful Queen Joan, the dreaded pirate Kheir-ed-Din Barbarossa, the ecstatic nun Serafina, the eccentric Sir Nathaniel Thorold, the treasure-hunting excavator Norbert Hadrawa, the South State colonel John Clay MacKowen, the cannon king Friedrich Alfred Krupp, the Baron Jacques d'Adelswärd Fersen, Lenin, Maxim Gorky, Norman Douglas, Axel Munthe, and many, many more.

This book concerns chiefly these peoples and others whose lives and works in one way or another are associated with Capri. For the sake of historical continuity, however, excursions in time and space are made into the world beyond this little island's waters. Only the most essential facts are given about Capri's geology in an extremely simplified form, and nothing is said about its flora and fauna. Nor is an attempt made to describe the island's fantastic rock formations, the bewitching light in the Blue Grotto, the breathtaking view across the Bay of Naples towards Vesuvius and the mountains of the Sorrento Peninsula, or any of the other wonders of nature: all these things have been depicted by countless authors and painters, although not even the best of them have succeeded in giving more than a weak reflection of reality. To aid in correct pronunciation, certain Greek, Latin and Italian names have been provided with accent in the index.

The illustrations portray primarily man-made works which are or have been on Capri: stone implements, ceramics, architecture, sculpture, and paintings. Nothing is shown of the island's scenery and people, pictured abundantly in other books. For the photographs used here I wish to thank: Donna Laetitia Cerio-Holt, Capri; Azienda Autonoma di Soggiorno e Turismo, Capri; the Soprintendenza alle Antichità delle Province di Napoli e Caserta, Naples; the German Archaeological Institute, Rome; the Département des Antiquités Grecques et Romaines, Musée du Louvre, Paris; and The Trustees of the British Museum, London.

It would have been difficult to write a book of this type anywhere else but on Capri where one can find even the rarest of publications and records concerning the island in the Centro Caprense, also where Naple's many libraries and archives are within easy reach, and where the possibility of checking what has been written still exists within certain limits. I am grateful that I have been able to spend some of the last years of my life on this delightful island.

Villa Ceselle, Anacapri, June, 1974

A. A.

PREFACE TO THE ENGLISH EDITION

This English edition of my book entitled « Capri, Från stenåldern till turiståldern », written in Swedish and published in 1975, has been made possible thanks to financial and editorial collaboration between the Foundation of Axel Munthe's San Michele and Professor Paul Åström, Publisher, Göteborg.

Thanks are also due to the Svenska Humanistiska Förbundet, assignee of the copyright of the Swedish edition, for permitting the publication of this English version.

The translation was made by Mrs. Carole Gillis, Lund. A necessary revision of her version has been carried out by myself; and in doing so, I have cancelled some passages of less interest for non-Scandinavian readers, and added or altered other paragraphs, with regard to literature which has appeared in later years (see Addenda, at the end of the Bibliography).

Lund, July 1979

A. A.

PREHISTORIC CAPRI

The Bay of Naples is bounded on the north and northeast by the dark volcano cone of Vesuvius, by the pitted crater fields called Campi Flegrei, by the Monte di Procida peninsula with the Cape of Misenum, and by the islands of Procida and Ischia. These formations are all of eruptive origin, consisting of grey-black lava or volcanic ash, either solidified into yellowish-brown tufa or still loose and grainy (which the Italians call pozzolana).

In the south, the Bay is limited by the grey limestone massif which forms the Sorrento Peninsula and creates the rocky island of Capri. These limestone mountains were formed in the sea through an unceasing, silent underwater rain of billions upon billions of dead calcareous algae and foraminifera which along with molluscs, coral polyps and other lime-producing salt water organisms accumulated in the depths for millions of years. This enormous deposit, compressed and cemented together into hard stone, has gradually been forced up towards and above the surface of the sea by the movement of the earth's crust; has been covered by new layers of limestone, clay and sandstone; has risen and fallen repeatedly, as shown by marks of erosion and shelves formed by waves on ancient shores; and has been shaken and reformed by tremendous eruptions from volcanoes long-since vanished into the sea, but whose ash can still be found here and there also on the limestone mountains in the form of soft tufa or loose pozzolana.

Formed by these slowly shaping or violently reshaping processes, Capri rises from the deep as one of the world's most fantastically beautiful islands, a rock of rugged and riddled

6

limestone, clad in green. It consists of a lower mid-section between two higher parts, both of which have, on almost every side, tremendous precipices, in which some sixty caves of various size are to be found. The eastern part reaches its greatest height, 334 meters (c. 1100 feet) above sea level, at its northeast elevation, and from this point, called Monte Tiberio, the ground sinks towards the southwest between three shorter peaks, Monte San Michele in the north, Monte Tuoro in the southeast, and Castiglione in the southwest. The western part, which is considerably larger, presents sheer cliffs towards the midsection and the southern coast, where it reaches its highest point, called Monte Solaro, 589 meters (c. 1930 feet) above sea level; and from these precipices, the terrain sinks towards the western coast, which is broken up by ravines and peninsulas. The lower mid-section, which conists of a mighty tufa embankment, slopes downward from a narrow east-west ridge called Due Mari towards the wider and lower shore in the north and a narrower and steeper one in the south. As far back as history goes, the low strip of coastline in the north which faces the Bay and the mainland has always been the foremost landing-place, and for larger vessels the only one, on the island. The narrow strip of coastline in the south, Marina Piccola, can protect only small fishing boats, and this is also the case for the small bay at the island's southeast point called Porto di Tragara.

The Greek geographer and historian Strabo, who wrote about the Mediterranean countries during the reign of Augustus, is of the opinion (6, 1, 6) that Capri and other islands that lie just beyond a mountain promontory, were separated from it at one time, whereas those islands which lie out in open waters must have risen up from the depths. That Strabo's conception is correct at least as far as Capri is concerned has been proven in modern times by the geological affinity between Capri and the mountains of the Sorrento Peninsula and through the palaeontological and archaeological discoveries made on the island.

Capri has the honour of being the first place, as far as we know, where remains of animals who vanished tens of thousands of years ago and traces of the activities of primitive stone age men were found.

The discovery was made two thousand years ago. The Roman historian Gaius Suetonius Tranquillus, c. 75-140 A.D., tells us in his biography of Augustus (Aug. 72, 3) that the emperor used to decorate his country estates not so much with statues and paintings but with porticos and parks, as well as with objects which were distinctive through their age and rarity: *qualia sunt Capreis immanium beluarum ferarumque membra praegrandia, quae dicuntur gigantum ossa, et arma heroum.* Suetonius has been read and commented on frequently throughout the ages. But what those things actually were which he names as the subject of Augustus' collecting activity, « such as on Capri, the enormous limbs of colossal monsters and beasts, which are called the bones of the giants, and the weapons of the heroes », could be ascertained to a certain extent only through the geological, archaeological and palaeontological discoveries made on the island in the 19th and early 20th centuries A.D.

When digging the foundations in 1905-06 for an extension of the Hotel Quisisana, situated in the town of Capri, at the beginning of the Tragara valley which extends southwards between Castiglione and Monte Tuoro, the excavators discovered a layer of eruptive material, 2.80 meter (c. 9 feet) thick, covered by a 1.70 meter (c. 5 1/2 - foot) thick layer of earth, and lying on a 2 to 5 meter (c. 6 1/2 to 16-foot) deep mass of red clay from a dried-up lake. In this clay, which rested on the living limestone rock, was found a large number of fossilized skeletal remains of huge mammals, belonging to extinct early quaternary species of, i.a., elephant, rhinoceros, hippopotamus, bear, and deer: *Elephas primigenius, Rhinoceros Merckii, Hippopotamus maior, Ursus spelaeus, Cervus elaphus.*

Dr. Ignazio Cerio, a physician well versed in natural sciences and archaeology, took charge of these fossils as well as artefacts of flint and quartzite, roughly worked to form the almond shape which is characteristic for the Chelléen period, the oldest phase of the palaeolithic period (early Stone Age) (Fig. 1). The finds were published by A. De Blasio and L. Pigorini after having been divided up between the Museo Preistorico in Rome, the Department of Anthropology, University of Naples, and Dr. Cerio's collection, which now belongs to the museum of the Centro Caprense, housed in the Palazzo Cerio at the piazza of the town of Capri.

Since neither those enormous mammals nor the primitive palaeolithic people who made and used the stone implements could in all probability have traversed a wide expanse of water, one must logically draw the conclusion that the rocks with their lakes and streams on which these beings lived, most likely during the last interglacial period, had not yet become an island but belonged to the Sorrento Peninsula.

Objections were raised, however, by scholars who either maintained that the stone artefacts of Chelléen type did not come from this excavation or doubted in any case that the palaeolithic people of Capri lived contemporaneously with the giant animals, since the artefacts according to Dr. Cerio's own observations were found only in the upper parts of the clay mass which contained the animal fossils. A new and scientifically controlled excavation was therefore carried out in the vicinity of the Quisisana where the same red clay, although without animal fossils, was found, with a layer of volcanic material above it containing Chelléen artefacts at the bottom.

We have thus uncontestable proof that human beings lived on what are now the rocks of Capri during the earliest phase of the palaeolithic age. The finds, on the other hand, give no proof that these men lived at the same time as the great animals, but incised figures of mammoths and cave bears made by palaeolithic man in other parts of Europe make this most likely. No remains of human skeletons were found at the Quisisana site, so we don't know to what extent the palaeolithic inhabitants of Capri resembled the primitive human type first discovered at Neanderthal, in Germany, and named after that place.

The violent volcanic eruptions which left the thick tufa embankment between Marina Grande and Marina Piccola, the almost 10-foot thick layer of eruptive material above the clay mass near the Quisisana, and the volcanic ash which was found even in the caves, washed there by the water, probably caused the demise of the giant beasts if they were not already extinct. If any descendants of the palaeolithic people survived these eruptions, the substantial subsidence and the almost as great elevation of the land, resulting in Capri's rocks being surrounded by water, they must have found their living conditions disastrously changed.

In all probability, therefore, the new island created by the terrific tellurian convulsions lay uninhabited for thousands of years, until that time in Europe when people possessing improved mental and physical abilities created the prerequisites for higher forms of civilization, above all by sowing, planting and domesticating animals for subsistance and clothing, instead of the haphazard gathering and hunting which ruled the palaeolithic man's life. At the same time, they learned also to form, decorate and fire pottery used for the preparation and storing of food and drink and to give their stone weapons and tools greated refinement and effectiveness by polishing and mounting them on shafts and handles. Capri has preserved numerous and significant traces of such activity from this period which we call the neolithic, or late Stone Age.

Already in the 1870's, Ignazio Cerio had taken charge of scattered objects stemming from the late Stone Age and the succeeding Bronze Age, among other things, a well-preserved bronze axe. Near Le Parate, on the central ridge of the island below Monte Solaro, he found, furthermore, over a thousand thin knives and scrapers of the black glass-like volcanic stone called obsidian. This find indicates that here, where now the roads to the town of Capri from Marina Grande, Anacapri and Marina Piccola converge, there was once a neolithic hut-village where these razor-sharp tools were produced. Similar obsidian tools and neolithic pottery sherds were later taken charge of by Antonino Mazzarella, mayor of Anacapri from 1914 to 1923, on the promontory on the western side of the island which is called Punta Campetiello. These finds prove that there were settlements scattered over the island in neolithic times.

Infinitely more abundant are the neolithic finds made in the Grotta delle Felci, « the Cave of the Ferns », which is an annex to the lofty Grotta dell'Arco which yawns in the cliff of Monte Solaro above Marina Piccola. In 1882, Ignazio Cerio excavated great amounts of prehistoric objects here which were presented to the Institute of Anthropology at the University of Naples and published in 1895 by A. De Blasio. Following new excavations in 1922 and 1923, the noted prehistorian U. Rellini presented a fundamental comparative study of the old and new finds from the cave. Lastly, certain finds in the cave have been studied by G. Buchner, on the basis of excavations made there in 1944.

Trodden down earth floors on different levels, with find and sterile layers inbetween, showed that the cave was a refuge for people for very long periods of time but also stood vacant at intervals. In addition to rough everyday pottery in all the habitation levels, there were found fine neolithic vases painted with linear patterns on a polychrome background (Fig. 1) and, in the upper layers, large amounts of a black polished pottery, smooth or decorated with incised geometric designs filled in with white (Fig. 2), a pottery which has its parallels on the Italian mainland and belongs to the Bronge Age. No objects made of the metal which gave its name to this age were found, with the exception of a bronze, or rather, copper dagger. This is not surprising, however, since both copper and tin, which man gradually learned to alloy in the right proportions to produce hard bronze, were expensive, imported metals. Thus, worn-out bronze utensils were melted down, and stone tools continued to be used to a large extent both during the Bronze Age and well into the Iron Age.

Stone weapons and tools were found in great quantity in the cave. Ignazio Cerio discovered around 200 axes, knives, saws and scrapers of obsidian, quartzite, diorite, jadeite and flint (Fig. 1), and an even larger number of chips and splinters from the same materials. This shows that the people in the cave carved these tools and weapons out of blocks which, since these materials are not native to Capri, must have been imported across the sea in primitive boats: obsidian from the volcanic Aeolian islands north of Sicily, flint from the Apennines, jadeite perhaps from the mountains of Liguria.

Bones from sheep, cattle and pigs, from deer and dogs, birds and fish, as well as shells of mussels and snails, gave evidence that the cave-dwellers took their primary nutrition, and probably their clothing, from domestic animals but supplemented their diet with what they could get from the sea and the wilderness of the island, and that here, as everywhere, the dog was man's companion and helper, Hearths with remains of charcoal and burnt animal bones proved that one had learned to strike and use a fire for the preparation of food.

In addition, some fifty oval and slightly concave sandstone blocks were found in the cave as well as a number of rough balls of limestone, both with clear signs of having been used to grind red ochre. Two such grinding stones with traces of red ochre were found together with rough pottery and human skeletal remains in a separate hole in the cave, indicating that the dead were buried with a certain amount of care and with such objects that they might need in the next world. Similar grinding stones and red-coloured skeletal remains from other neolithic burials show that red ochre was used to colour the dead, and perhaps even the living, probably in connection with religious rites pertaining to funerals and death cult.

Elsewhere in the cave, as well, many scattered remains of human skeletons were found: a lower jawbone from a child suffering from rickets, a fragmentary jawbone from a man in his 70's which showed evidence of having been adapted for use as a polishing tool, and bones which were cracked, scraped hollow, and chared. It is uncertain whether these remains should be interpreted as a sign that one put bones from old graves to some use or that cannibalism was practiced. If the latter was the case, one can probably assume that those who were eaten were enemies from other parts of the island or from the mainland.

Because of the large number of grinding stones and the limited space in the cave, Buchner has come to the conclusion that during the neolithic period it was not used for habitation but as a sacred cult and burial place. This seems to be confirmed by another curious find in the cave: two oval limestones, rounded by the waves, on which are painted very schematic human figures similar to those known from palaeolithic sites in France, Spain, Liguria, and on the island of Levanzo, near the west coast of Sicily. Buchner regards these painted stones as cult objects giving witness to traditions from late palaeolithic times.

These discoveries, which during the last hundred years have given us such insight into Capri's past, have also helped us to understand Suetonius' comments about the curious interests of Augustus as a collector. One can no longer doubt, as some did earlier, that the « enormous limbs of colossal monsters and beasts » which were on view in the Emperor's collection on Capri, and which were popularly called « the bones of the giants », really were found on the island. They must have been skeletal parts of huge extinct animals similar to those unearthed in 1905 at Quisisana. Since these remains lay at a depth of about 16 to 32 feet (5 to 10 meters) below the present surface of the ground, it is probable that the bones which Augustus collected were discovered while digging the foundations for one of the Emperor's palaces on the island.

It is more difficult to determine what Suetonius meant by the expression « the weapons of the heroes ». One might logically assume that palaeolithic artefacts could have been found together with the huge bones during such excavations, as nineteen centuries later at the Quisisana. But it seems hardly likely that even learned and observant men at that time, acquainted with Lucretius' conception (De Rerum Natura, 5, 975) of a prehistoric age in which men lived in caves and hunted with stones and clubs, were able to see that such roughly chipped stones were formed by man; and it is even less likely that they would call them « the weapons of the heroes ». One has assumed with greater reason that these « heroes' weapons » were bronze axes and/or finely polished neolithic stone axes similar to those found in the Grotta delle Felci. This was refuted, however, by the French archaeologist Salomon Reinach, who maintained that such stone axes were called *cerauniae* by the Romans, which means 'lightning stones', since they were thought to originate from places struck by lightning. Further he thought that the comma which in modern editions of Suetonius is put after « the bones of the giants » should be removed, thereby making the author declare that these huge remains were said to be not only the « bones of the giants » but also « the weapons of the heroes ».

Reinach's reasoning, however, is untenable for two reasons. In the first place, it is stated quite clearly in Pliny's Naturalis Historia (37, 134-135) that *cerauniae* was the collective name for a number of crystalline gems which appeared in various shapes and colours and to which was often attributed magical power: there were white *cerauniae* sparkling with blue; matt ones; black and round, which guaranteed success in war; red, long and axe-formed ones which were particularly called *cerauniae;* and a rare type, not specifically described, which was sought by the magicians because it was found only where lightning had struck. In the second place, it must be considered highly unlikely that the skeletal remains in question could have been construed, even by the most unknowledgable discoverer, as being both bones from the mythical giants and weapons of ancient heroes.

Since Suetonius expressly indicates Augustus' interest in collecting objects distinctive through their age and rarity and

14

gives the finds on Capri as examples of similar things, it is highly probable that the Emperor collected what unlearned people termed « bones of giants » fully aware not only that these bones belonged to « colossal monsters and beasts » but also that these animals lived a very long time ago. For the same reason, it is believable that he also incorporated axes and daggers of bronze and polished stone in his collection and in them saw weapons used in times long past. Naturally, he had no way of knowing that these giant beasts lived many tens of thousands of years before and that the weapons were produced by men who lived a primitive life and were perhaps cannibals. The beautiful shapes of these objects more likely carried his thoughts back to the forgotten pre-Homeric heroes living unsung before Agamemnon, those of whom Horace talks in a famous ode (4, 9):

Vixere fortes ante Agamemnona.

GREEK CAPRI

In Books IX to XII of the Odyssey, the cunning Odysseus, after having been cast naked upon the shores of the island of the Phaeacians by a storm, recounts his perilous adventures after the fall of Troy for the King and his court. He narrates how he had to forcibly remove his crew from the land of the Lotus-eaters after they ate the delicious lotus fruit and instantly lost all desire to continue the journey home; further, how he saved himself and his remaining men from the one-eyed, man-eating Cyclops Polyphemus by blinding him with a red-hot stake; how he arrived at the island of Aeolus, the king of the winds, and received a sealed bag from him containing all the winds except the favourable west wind; how the wild Laestrygonians, also man-eating giants, hurled boulders down on his fleet, crushing all the ships except his own; how thanks to Hermes' magic herb, he was able to avoid the fate which overtook his men on the island of Aeaea when Circe, the daughter of the Sun, turned them into swine; how he came to the Cimmerians, living in a state of eternal night, and met the shades of the dead in Hades; how he heard the song of the Sirenes but managed to withstand their enticements by blocking his rowers' ears with wax and having himself tied to the mast; and how after a fearful journey in sailing between the monsters Scylla and Charybdis, he arrived at the island of Thrinakie, where his final misfortune was being prepared. For during his absence, his men slaughtered and devoured the Sun's holy oxen pasturing on this island, and as punishment, his ship and the last of his crew were destroyed at sea by a thunderbolt thrown by Zeus. Odysseus alone escaped and drifted to the island of the nymph Calypso, who kept him as a loved prisoner in her cave for seven years.

The lovesick Calypso, the sorcerous Circe, the king of the winds Aeolus, the Lotus-eaters, the Cyclopes, the Laestrygonians and Cimmerians, the twelve-footed Scylla who with her six sharptoothed heads on their long necks seized six of Odysseus' best men, the invisible Charybdis who three times daily sucked down the salt sea water and as many times spewed it up again, the dreaded Sirenes who with their irresistibly enticing song lured sailors to their flowering fields strewn with the ghastly remains of their victims: thanks to Homer, all of these fantastic creations have become immortal.

Archaeological discoveries during the last hundred years show that the legends about the Trojan war, Agamemnon's golden Mycenae, King Nestor's Pylos and King Minos' Knossos mirror a historical reality belonging to the Bronze Age civilization of Crete and of the Greek mainland during the second millennium B.C.

In the same way, the discoveries of the last few decades have made it clear that even the incredible adventures described in the Odyssey had ties with the world of reality. Through place names and literary tradition, the majority of Odysseus' adventures can be linked to Sicily and the western coast of southern Italy. An ancient commentator on Apollonius Rhodius' Argonautica (3, 311) states that according to Hesiod, writing around 700 B.C., Circe arrived at her island near Tyrrhenia in the chariot of the Sun. Tyrrhenia was the name given by the Greeks to the land inhabited by the people they called tyrrhenoi or tyrsenoi, and whom the Romans called Etrusci. During the Archaic period, the Etruscans reigned over a territory that stretched from their homeland, Etruria, into the Po valley in the north and into Latium and Campania in the south. Circe's island has been identified as the mountain promontory in Latium called Circeii, which according to Pliny's Naturalis Historia (3, 57) was once an island. To this day, it bears its ancient name, italianized: Monte Circeo. Strabo (5, 3, 6) states that it looked like an island, surrounded as it was by water and marshes, and that there was a little town and a temple to Circe as well as a bowl which was said to have belonged to Odysseus.

The land of the Cimmerians and the place where Odysseus met the dead in Hades has been placed in that region west of Naples which is called Campi Flegrei, « the burning fields ». In one of his plays, now lost, Sophocles spoke of an oracle of the dead near the « Tyrsenian Sea », by which he meant undoubtedly the crater lake north of Monte di Procida called Aornos or Lacus Avernus, and which today is known as Lago d'Averno. Strabo describes the region in detail (5, 4, 5-6), saying that steaming and water-filled volcanic craters, dark forests and hot or cold springs easily gave rise to the belief that here was an entrance to the underworld and that the water came from its rivers, the dark Styx and the flaming Pyriflegeton.

As for the Sirenes, we learn from ancient commentators on Apollonius (4, 892) that according to Hesiod they were three in number and lived on the island of Anthemoessa. The name means « the flowering » and brings to mind the *leimon anthemoeis,* the flower meadow of the Sirenes, mentioned in the Odyssey. Strabo, however, who has an interesting interpretation of poetry and reality in the Odyssey, cites other traditions and spokesmen (1, 2, 11 ff.; cf. 5, 4, 8), who placed the home of the Sirenes in various locations by or near the west coast of southern Italy: on Pelorias, now Capo Peloro, Sicily's northwest promontory north of Messina, or on the point of the Sorrento Peninsula, where there was a temple to Athena, said to have been founded by Odysseus, and a sanctuary to the Sirenes. This explains why the point was called both Athenaion and Seirenoussa. The Roman geographer Pomponius Mela in his De Chorographia (2, 69) describes three rocky, uninhabited islets off the southern coast of the Peninsula as *petrae quas sirenes habitarunt,* « the rocks where the Sirenes lived »; they were called therefore, according to Strabo (1, 2, 12) Seirenes, « the Sirenes ». They are now called Li Galli, « the Roosters ». It is tempting to regard this name as derived from some con-

18

fused tradition concerning the featnered musical beings which were once supposed to have lived there. But Norman Douglas states that the name appears as « Guallo » in a 12th century chronicle and is most likely connected with a family name. Strabo also mentions (5, 4, 7) that there was a grave monument in Neapolis erected in memory of Parthenope, one of the Sirenes, and (6, 1, 1) that the little island of Leukosia, situated south of Paestum, took the name of another Siren who was washed ashore and buried there after all the Sirenes had flung themselves into the sea and drowned. Some ancient commentators say that they did this out of chagrin over not succeeding in luring Odysseus to them. In his Naturalis Historia (3, 62, and 3, 85) Pliny gives similar information about these beings.

Servius gives a different version of the Sirenes in his comments on Virgil's Aeneid, 5, 864. He says that according to the fable there were three of them, half bird, half young woman. One sang, another played the flute, and the third played the lyre. They lived first near Pelorias, then on Capreae, and lured sailors to destruction with their singing. Servius, however, gives a rational explanation for them by saying that they were actually harlots who caused seamen economic ruin and therefore were said to cause shipwrecks.

Servius is a late author, writing his commentaries probably during the second half of the 4th century A.D. This is no reason, however, for considering his placing of the Sirenes on Capri to be an untrustworthy invention. In all likelihood, he took it from some treatise now lost which he does not mention. He might have been given the idea that they were harlots from the Greek grammarian Herakleitos (3rd century B.C.), who in his work about incredible things, Peri Apiston (14), describes the Sirenes as beautiful and delightfully singing hetaerae, who were thought to be shaped like women with birds' legs.

Near Marina Piccola there is a small rock jutting into the sea which is called Sirena or Scoglio delle Sirene. But this name cannot be adduced in support of Capri's claim to have been the home of the Sirenes, for it is probably an invention by some fanciful 18th century scholar well read in his Servius. On the other hand, it is quite natural that the Sirenes were considered to have lived on Capri, for the inviting green spread between the dangerous precipices of this island tallies much better with the flowering Siren meadow of Homer and the blooming Siren island of Hesiod than the rocky cape of the Sorrento Peninsula and the barren islets of Li Galli.

Strabo (6, 1, 5) indicates the islands of Lipari north of Sicily as the home of Aeolus. These islands were also called Aeoliae and even today are referred to as Isole Eolie. The island Thrinakie, « Trident island », was already in antiquity considered to be Sicily. Scylla and Charybdis were placed on opposite sides of the straits running between Sicily and the mainland. Strabo states (1, 2, 16) that Charybdis' activities can be equated with the current in the strait and cites Polybius who says that Homer's depiction of Scylla as a monster snatching up dolphins, sharks and other large sea creatures quite accurately describes the wealth of underwater life teaming in the Straits where then as now, swordfish were caught off the promontory called Scyllaion, now Scilla, north of Reggio Calabria. The Cyclopes and the Laestrygonians were also placed on Sicily. According to a tradition mentioned by Thucydides (6, 2, 1), the Laestrygonians were thought to have been the earliest inhabitants of the island. Even today a bay called Porto d'Ulisse and three small islands named Isole dei Ciclopi north of Catania recall the *portus Ulixis,* Odysseus' harbour, and the *scopuli tres Cyclopum,* the three rocks of the Cyclopes, named in Pliny's Naturalis Historia (3, 89). Pliny says further that the Laestrygonian fields, *Laestrygonii campi,* extended just beyond. Earlier in the same work (3, 59), however, he cites another tradition which placed the Laestrygonians near Formiae.

The inventiveness of the Greeks knew no bounds and it is no use trying to find consistency and system in their myths. But the fact that so many ancient authors from the time of Hesiod onwards, albeit with some variations, indicated the west coast of southern Italy and the east coast of Sicily as the setting for many of Odysseus' adventures seems to imply the existence of old traditions concerning the perils incurred during early travels to unknown shores in the west. Shores where fire-breathing mountains and frightening cliffs, dark forests and secret caves, breakers and whirlpools, giant squids and other sea monsters set the seafarers' immagination spinning and sowed the seeds for many a seaman's tale, ultimately resulting in a large and immortal epic poem.

That Odysseus, in fact, is a legendary representative for early, daring Greek seafarers who sailed west to Sicily and to the peninsula later called Italia, is proved by archaeology. Decorated Helladic and Mycenaean vases and sherds, sometimes with Mycenaean writing, as well as Mycenaean bronze weapons, gold rings and necklaces have come to light in recent years during excavations on the Aeolian Islands and in many places around Siracusa and Catania, near Agrigento, around Taranto, on Ischia and even as far north as in Etruria, which give testimony to numerous Greek trading voyages in the west during the Aegean Bronze Age, between 1800 and 1200 B.C.

The decline and fall of the Myceneaen Bronze Age civilization around 1200 B.C. was followed by a dark age of turbulence, migration and strife. This cultural twilight was marked by the disappearance of the Mycenaean form of writing and by a deterioration in the decoration of Mycenaean pottery, which was primarily inspired by nature, but had later become more and more stylized. Only after the lapse of some centuries was a new Greek civilization gradually developed, with a formal, geometric style of decoration, and with a new writing system derived from Phoenician signs adapted to form the alphabet which, in its Latin form, has come to be used all over the world.

The enormous potential of the new Hellenic civilization was evidenced in spiritual and material activities of immense historical significance. Driven by economic difficulties and social wrongs, by thirst for adventure and profit, the Greeks in the course of the 8th century B.C. began to set sail across the seas in all directions, going as mercenaries to Egypt, as traders to familiar as well as unknown countries, and as colonists to such coastal areas along the Mediterranean and the Black Sea where the inhabitants were unable to prevent them from founding new Greek city-states. These emigrations were organized by cities in the mother country advanced in production and export: primarily Miletus, Corinth, Chalcis, Rhodes, the early Sparta, and the territory known as Achaia. From these Hellenic outposts, Greek civilization spread to Thracians and Scythians, to Etruscans and Italic tribes, to the Celts in what in now France, and to other *bárbaroi,* so called by the Greeks because of the harsh and incomprehensible languages they spoke.

The most important of the Greek colony cities were those which were established along the coasts of southern Italy, washed by the Ionian and Tyrrhenian Seas, and around Sicily, with the exception of the western tip of the island, which was controlled by the Carthaginians. With the brilliant courts of their tyrants, with their schools of philosophy, their poets, artists and scientists, their heroic struggle against the Carthaginians and their bitter internal feuds, these Greek cities and the areas they controlled appeared as a new, bigger, richer and more powerful Hellas, a « Hellás Megále », which even under Roman control managed to retain its Greek culture and language, and its old name, latinized: Magna Graecia. The greatness of Hellás Megále manifests itself even today in the mighty ruins of temples and fortifications, which despite earthquakes and their having been used as quarries may still be seen in Paestum, Velia and Metapontum, in Syracuse and Gela, in Agrigento and Selinunte. The civilization of the Greek colonies of Sicily and southern Italy was also to be of major importance to the world because of the cultural influence it had on Rome, first indirectly through the Etruscans, and later through direct contact.

The fact that several of the most important Greek colonies in the West were founded in regions where Mycenaean traders had been active centuries before makes it more than likely that the colonists, to a certain extent, were guided by narrations passed down through the centuries concerning the Mycenaeans' travels in the same areas. This may also explain why the first colonists, men from Chalcis, Eretria and Kyme on the long island of Euboea, ventured to brave the Etruscan fleets — pirate fleets, according to Strabo (6, 2, 2) — on the Tyrrhenian Sea, in order to settle at a place far north which they obviously considered advantageous, for more than one reason.

Livy states (8, 22, 5-6) that the colonists first settled on the islands of Aenaria and Pithecusae, and later founded the city of Cumae (the Greek Kyme) on the mainland. Strabo says expressly (5, 4, 4) that this was the oldest of all the Greek cities both on Sicily and the Italian mainland, but he also mentions (5, 4, 9) the settlement on fertile Pithekoussai, adding that the colonists abandoned it owing to internal conflicts and the volcanic activity of the island. Pithekoussai is the island which the Romans called Aenaria, now Ischia; but when Livy speaks of Aenaria and Pithecusae as two separate islands, perhaps he was thinking of Aenaria and Prochyta, that is, Ischia and the small island of Procida, which the colonists could hardly have dared to leave unoccupied. Kyme, called Cumae by the Romans, had its acropolis on a sheer cliff near the sandy coast north of the promontory of Monte Procida. Archaeological excavations carried out on Ischia since 1952 by G. Buchner and much earlier in Cumae by E. Gàbrici have confirmed the veracity of the literary sources and established the date of the Greek settlement on Ischia as the first half of the 8th century B.C., somewhat earlier than the founding of Kyme, followed in time by the Chalcidian colony Naxos, the Corinthian Syrakousai, the Achaean Sybaris and Kroton, and the Spartan Taras, called by the Romans Tarentum, and today, Táranto.

The colonists who settled on Ischia did so primarily, as Strabo implies, because of the island's fertility, but in all probability also to have a protected base from which attacks could be made on the nearby mainland, to which they were attracted by its rich fertile plains, inhabited by a people called *opikoi* by the Greeks, Osci in Latin. The first step was taken with the founding of Kyme-Cumae. The Cumaeans in the course of time acquired what they were lacking on their own sandy shore, namely a natural harbour on the other side of the Misenum promontory, in a town called Dikaiarcheia, which the Romans renamed Puteoli, and which is now called Pozzuoli. Further east on the wide bay, which once was named after Kyme but was also called the « Krater », the « Wine Bowl », because of its shape and the fertility of its shores, the Cumaeans founded a city which, according to Strabo (5, 4, 7), later received a supplement of new immigrants from Chalcis, Pithekoussai and Athens, which is why it was called Nea Polis, « New City », as opposed to the original city Palaeopolis, « Old City », mentioned by Livy (8, 22).

Most probably the colonists on Ischia and in Kyme had one more reason for their bold advance northward, and that was their desire to be close to be big Etruscan cities, principally Caere, Tarquinii and Vulci. These cities, it is true, did not allow foreign colonization on their territories but wellcomed Greek merchants and artists; and from the time of the foundation of Kyme the Etruscans constituted one of the biggest markets for Greek pottery, exchanging it for iron ore from Elba, as finds from Ischia seem to indicate.

Whether Mycenaean Greeks during their trading voyages to the West left any wares on Capri is unknown, for no objects of Mycenaean character have been found there, as far as we know. Nor have any traces of Iron Age burials like those found all over the Italian mainland been brought to light on the island. Agreeing with the opinion of the archaeologist F. von Duhn, who thought that the region around the Bay of Naples, except for Ischia and Cumae, was depopulated for seven or eight hundred years after the 18th century B.C. because of Vesuvius' violent activity during that period, the volcanologist I. Friedländer interpreted the absence on Capri of finds of the type mentioned as a sign that this island, too, was uninhabited during the same space of time.

This conclusion, however, is not convincing. Capri is scarcely closer to Vesuvius than Ischia is, where Mycenaean pottery from the 14th century B.C. discovered in native graves indicate that the latter island was populated then. Thus, there is no reason *a priori* to believe that Capri was depopulated because of Vesuvius' eruptions. And the fact that finds similar to those discovered on Ischia have not been recorded on Capri does not necessarily mean that such finds could not have been brought to light there by persons who did not understand their importance and did not take care of them. To draw conclusions *ex silentio* is risky when one does not have a large and well-checked archaeological material at one's disposal.

We do not know much about the role that Capri played in the history of Greek colonization either. In Virgil's Aeneid (7, 733-736), one of Aeneas' enemies is Oebalus, son of Telon, king of the Teleboans on Capreae and ruler over a large part of Campania. These Teleboans, the « far-shouting », are mentioned in Hesiod's poem about Heracles' shield (19) in connection with the Taphians, inhabitants of the island of Taphos near Acarnania, the region of north-west Greece facing the islands of Cephallonia, Leucas, and Odysseus' Ithaca. According to Aristotle, cited by Strabo (7, 7, 2; cf. 10, 2, 20), these Teleboans also lived in Acarnania.

In the first edition of his work Campanien, published in 1879, the German historian J. Beloch held the view that these traditions mirrored an actual emigration by Teleboans from Acarnania to Capri, since the first Greek voyages to Italy, for geographical reasons, must have started from western Greece: Capri was thus the first place in Campania, and perhaps on the whole west coast of Italy, to be settled by Greek colonists, who later on colonized Campania; while the colonists from Chalcis and Corinth merely followed in the track of the Acarnanians. This idea, however, is in direct opposition to what ancient historians tell us about Greek colonization in the West, as well as to the results of later archaeological research. In the second edition of his work (1890), Beloch rightly discarded his previous idea and relegated the whole story about Teleboans on Capri to the realm of myth. In any case, even if an emigration from Acarnania to Capri is not unthinkable, Telon and Oebalus ought not to be more historical than King Capreus who, according to an anonymous commentator on Virgil called *Servius auctus,* gave Capri its name — despite the fact that, according to a sermon transcribed in 1174 about the patron saint of Capri, *Sermo de transitu Sancti Constantii,* the tomb of King Telon was still to be seen in medieval times. In the Greek colonies it was customary to erect grave memorials and sanctuaries for the cult of real or mythical city founders. King Telon's tomb on Capri was probably just as authentic as that of the Siren Parthenope in Naples.

In his book about Capri (1938), I. Friedländer oddly enough adopts Beloch's old discarded theory, saying that the Greek colonists most likely settled on Capri earlier than on the mainland. He tries to strengthen his argument by stating that the oldest Greek pottery found on the island consists of geometric vases from the 10th century B.C. This statement is repeated by H. Kesel, with the difference that he ascribes these geometric vases to the 8th century B.C. These vases, however, are apocryphal, since to our knoledge no geometric pottery has ever been found on Capri. We have to admit that we have no means to establish from where and when the first Greek settlers arrived at Capri.

According to a quotation from the geographical encyclopedia called Ethniká, written by the Byzantine grammarian Stephanos, and now for the most part lost, Capri was mentioned in a geographical work by Hecataeus of Miletus, already in the 6th century B.C. This information, however, has been viewed with suspicion, since Καπρίη in Stephanos is followed by the explanation νῆσος Ἰταλίας, ' an island off Italy ', for in Hecataeus' time, ' Italia ' referred only to the toe of the Apennine peninsula.

It is also uncertain if the island got its name from the Greeks, who called it Kapríe, Kapría, Kapréa, or usually, in the plural, Kapríai, Kapréai, or if this name, in Latin Capreae, reflects a pre-Greek form, Italic or possibly Etruscan, or if it is perchance Phoenician.

This latter possibility was asserted by Giacomo Martorelli, an 18th century scholar with a passion for wild etymologies, in an odd work with the peculiar title De Regia Theca Calamaria, 'From the Royal Inkhouse' (1756). He was of the opinion that Cumae, Parthenope-Neapolis and other places around the Bay received their names from the Phoenicians, and further, that Capreae stemmed from the Phoenician *capraim,* ' two towns ' — which would fit in quite vell with Strabo's information (see below) about there having been two small towns on the island. Martorelli's theories won support at a time when scholars were intent on tracing Phoenicians almost everywhere in and outside of the Mediterranean. R. Mangoni and A. Canale were convinced that Capri was inhabited by Phoenicians before the arrival of the Teleboans, and even such an erudite scholar as Norman Douglas speaks of Phoenicians on Capri and their defeat at Cumae, obviously confusing them with the Etruscans and their débacle in 474 B.C. The ' Phoenician Steps ' must have been given their misleading name by some phoenicomaniac; for Mangoni they were still simply *l'antica scala.* The speculations of Martorelli and his followers contradict all historical facts and are considered now as being merely scholarly curiosities. The Phoenicians surely had trade connections with Sicily and the Apennine peninsula but never any colonies there. Their African colony Carthage established colonies on western Sicily, Sardinia and Corsica, but never by the Bay of Naples.

The assertion that the name Capreae was of Etruscan origin, first presented by B. Quaranta in Le antiche ruine di Capri, 1855, was accepted by Friedländer and considered « suggestive » by Norman Douglas. Quaranta based his statement on, i.a., the lexicographer Hesychius, who says that the Tyr-

rhenian word for goat was *kapra.* But, providing that Hesychius' information is correct, one may suspect that *kapra* was
one of the numerous Latin loan-words in the Etruscan language,
since the goat is called *capra* in Latin. To be sure, a *capra* does
appear in Etruscan inscriptions, but most likely it means ' vessel ', ' cinerary urn ', and can hardly be connected with the
name Capreae. Theoretically speaking, an Etruscan origin of
the name might be conceivable if those linguists are right who,
on the base of certain place-names, claim the existence of a
pre-Indo-European, ' Tyrrhenian ' language extended over the
whole Apennine peninsula in prehistoric times. The Etruscans
of historical times, it is true, are said to have gained control,
from Capua and other colonies founded by them — twelve in
number, according to Strabo (5, 4, 3) — over the inland of
Campania down to the river Silaris, now Sele north of Paestum.
This is confirmed by the fact that one of the longest Etruscan
inscriptions preserved has come to light in Capua and other,
shorter ones, at the temple of Apollo in Pompeii. But the
Greeks ruled Campania's coast and coastal waters from Cumae
and its daughter-cities. The Etruscans, therefore, tried to establish a base for their fleets by attacking Cumae, by land in 524
B.C. and by sea fifty years later. Both attempts failed, the
second one due to the intervention of Hiero I, ruler of Syracuse, with disastrous consequences for the Etruscan sea power.
This situation makes it, *a priori,* completely unlikely that the
Etruscans ever ruled Capri. No ancient author has ever implied
such a thing, and no monuments of Etruscan type, as far as is
known, have ever been discovered on the island.

If the name Capreae is thought to be associated with an
Italic word corresponding to the Latin *capra,* it ought to mean
' Goat Island '. Perhaps the island was rich in goats; the name
Tragara seems to be connected to the Greek *trágos,* he-goat.
But if the Greek colonists named this place, they may of course
also have given the whole island its name. In that case it
should be linked to the Greek *kápros,* meaning ' Boar Island ',
a name motivated perhaps by the possible abundance of wild

boars or by the shape of the island, showing a depression between two heights which, seen from the Bay, may have reminded the colonists of the notch in the boar's bristly back, always to be seen in ancient Greek representations of this animal. Most likely, however, we are dealing with a pre-Indo-European name which the Italic tribes perhaps connected with *capra,* the Greek with *kápros* — if they thought about it at all.

Strabo mentions briefly (5, 4, 9) that Kapréai had two small towns in ancient times, but later on only one. He adds that the Neapolitans took possession of this island too; but after having lost Pithekoussai in a war, they were given it back by Caesar Augustus, who made Kapréai his property and erected buildings there.

What Strabo meant in his first somewhat cryptic statement has long been the object of various interpretations. It is certain that one of these two small towns lay where the present town of Capri is, since a length of a city wall of archaic date, built of large irregular blocks and reinforced with regular ashlars, still exists and is partially visible between the piazza and the red ex-hotel Ercolano (Fig. 3), while other remains of the same wall were previously to be seen along the stretch now demarcated by Via Roma and at Via Castello on the west slope of Castiglione. This fortified town was no doubt the capital of Capri and bore the same name as the island, just as many Greek islands and their chief towns had the same name, for instance Rhodes, Samos, Chios, Thasos, and Leucas.

Opinions vary, on the other hand, concerning the question of where the other little town was situated and what Strabo meant by saying that « later on », that is, in his own time, there was only one town on Capri. Quaranta thought that this other town was somewhere down by the harbour. Norman Douglas concurred, being of the opinion that the old town within the walls had been abandoned in Strabo's time, that Anacapri should not be considered, and that the « Phoenician Steps » were probably built by Augustus.

The prominent archaeologist A. Maiuri and many others have interpreted Strabo's words to mean that the two small towns were forerunners to the later communities Capri and Anacapri, and that these towns came under a common rule when the island became imperial property.

Considering the many remains of ancient constructions found on the slope between the town of Capri and Marina Grande, H. Kesel has recently defended the old idea that Strabo's two small towns were identifiable with the upper, fortified settlement between Castiglione and Monte San Michele and the lower, unfortified one above Marina Grande. The latter, according to Kesel, had extended itself up the slope, so that in Strabo's time one could speak of one single town. The name Anacapri, says Kesel, which does not appear in ancient sources and is first to be found in 10th century Amalfi documents, does not refer to some ancient town, since no remains of such a settlement have come to light in Anacapri, but to the entire western part of the island, which was uninhabited during the Greek period and boasted little more than the imperial villas during the Roman era. During the Middle Ages, this outlying part bore the distorted name of Terra di Anna Crapa, often misunderstood and deformed into Donna Crapa.

These arguments, however, are far from convincing. It is highly unlikely, *a priori,* that the Greeks on Capri, during the turbulent centuries when Rome was fighting for control of Italy, its islands and coastal waters, would have dared to settle by the harbour in sufficient number to constitute a town. The remains of ancient constructions which have come to light between Marina Grande and the town of Capri are all from the time of the Roman Empire, when people dared to move down to coasts and plains from their lofty fortified cities. The name Anacapri, written as Anocapri in some old documents, indicates through its Greek prefix an « Upper Capri », hardly as opposed to the island in general but reasonably to the town of Capri. That it is not mentioned in the ancient literature available to us does not prove that it came into use only in the Middle Ages through Byzantine influence, and then to designate the whole western part of the island. On the contrary, the name Terra di Anna Crapa, « Anacapri's Territory », implies the existence of a medieval community which had preserved its old Greek name in distorted form. The fact that no remains of Greek buildings, as far as we know, have come to light in present-day Anacapri does not prove anything either, for what may have survived of such a community, probably small and because of its safe location unfortified, has of course been destroyed or hidden by the continuous building activity of later centuries. This is exactly what has occurred in the town of Capri, where all traces of the Greek settlement have disappeared, except for the sparse remains of the fortification wall, which for obvious reasons was kept in good condition for a long time.

But the strongest argument in favour of the theory that the second of Strabo's two small towns was a forerunner to Anacapri is the existence of the « Phoenician Steps » which, partly hewn out of the cliff, zigzag up the steep mountain from the harbour to Anacapri (Fig. 4). The number of the steps varies in various authors, from Fabio Giordano, who speaks of « around 600 », to Axel Munthe who prefers the magical number 777. Saying that there are more than 500, you are not exaggerating nor yielding to imagination. There is, however, not much left of the original steps, which is not surprising considering that for innumerable centuries they were the only connection by land between Anacapri and Marina Grande and thus had to be repaired uncountable times. Capaccio writes that Anacapri is reached *angusto, acclivi per gradus difficile ascensu, qui facillimus accolis exercitatione redditus est, dum etiam onera portant.* His description of the « narrow, steep and difficult stepped ascent, which by training has become quite easy for the inhabitants, even when they are bearing burdens », gives us an idea of a patience and a vigour which have vanished in our age of cars and asphalt roads. As already pointed out, these steps cannot have been made by the

Phoenicians. Nor have they any similarity to Roman roads and stairs, but obviously, as pointed out by Maiuri, to the steps made by the Greeks from immemorial times on the rocky islands of the Aegean. The « Phoenician Steps » are without doubt the work of the Greek colonists on Capri. But it is not reasonable to assume that these Greeks would have undertaken the long and toilsome task of creating this passage between the harbour and the elevated western part of the island if this part was only wasteland, a wilderness accessible to hunters and shepherds either by the path, now called Il Passatiello, which goes up Monte Santa Maria's eastern precipices from Le Parate, or by boat to the low Punta Carena, the southwest point of the island, or to the mouths of the ravines which sink towards the sea on its west coast.

Consequently, there is good reason for Anacapri to claim to be the forerunner of the second of Strabo's two small towns. On the other hand, it is hardly believable that Strabo's statement that « later on » there was only one town on the island can be explained with the supposition that the two towns vere united under common rule during the Roman Empire. It is more credible that the people living in the upper town in Roman times felt it so bothersome that many of them moved down to the lower town and its harbour. Thus Strabo could say with good reason that there was only one real town on the island.

We know nothing about the life of the Greek colonists and their early descendants on Capri. They probably lived a rather isolated life, secure behind their strong wall in the town of Kapréai and up in Anakapréai, above the long and arduous flight of steps. They must have seen ships sailing by on their way to Kyme or to the ports of Caere, Tarquinii and Vulci loaded with painted vases from Rhodes, Corinth, Sparta, Chalcis and Athens, vases which ended up in thousands in Etruscan graves, and later on in European and American museums. They might have seen the ships bearing Phocaeans of Asia Minor fleeing from the Persians around 540 B.C. to settle on Corsica, both on their way north and later retreating south, having been put to rout by the Etruscan and Carthaginian fleets. In 474 B.C. they might have watched the fleet of Hiero I of Syracuse as it headed north towards Kyme to prevent the Etruscans from conquering the city, and then on its return voyage loaded with booty after having crushed the Etruscan sea power and left a garrison on Pithekoussai.

The Greeks on Capri probably had very little or nothing to do with these trading vessels, emigration ships and Syracusan warships. Naturally, though, some Greek export items did end up on the island. G.M. Secondo mentions that « many Etruscan vases, some bronze candelabras and many clay lamps » were found around 1740 in a place called Torra above the church of San Costanzo. The bronze candelabra could have come from Etruscan workshops, which exported such products even to Greece. The « Etruscan » vases, on the other hand, were most likely Greek, for in the 18th century it was generally believed that the painted black figure and red figure clay vases found in Etruscan tombs were manufactured in Etruria, until Luigi Lanzi, in 1806, made it clear that they were imported from Greece. Mangoni states, further, that shortly after 1830 some Italo-Greek vases with red figures on black ground were found in the ancient necropolis near Le Parate.

It is probable that the Greeks on Capri were not greatly in touch with what was happening on the mainland, where, fifty years after the sea battle at Kyme, the warlike Samnites, a people of the mountains akin to the Oscans, captured the Etruscan city of Capua and shortly afterwards the Greek cities of Kyme and Dikaiarcheia, forcing themselves to be received as citizens also in Naples.

The Samnites, however, as is seen especially in Pompeii, were very soon hellenized; and at last they experienced defeat themselves at the hands of the Romans who, through bloody wars with Etruscans and Gauls, with the Tarentines and King Pyrrhus, the Carthaginians and Hannibal, on the Iberian peninsula and in Gallia, in Africa, Macedonia, Greece, Asia Minor and Syria, gained supremacy over Italy and finally over the whole Mediterranean world.

But the Roman conquerors, already influenced by Greek civilization as transmitted through the Etruscans, were completely conquered by it through their being acquainted with Greek literature after the war against the Tarentines and Pyrrhus (282-272 B.C.) and with Greek art during the second Punic war through the booty from Syrakousai (210 B.C.) and from Tarentum (209 B.C.). Rome's conquest of the Greek world brought about a strengthening and a renewed vast diffusion of Greek civilization.

In the regions of the old colonies in Sicily and southern Italy, Greek language and Greek civilization survived during the centuries of Roman domination. Strabo says (5, 4, 4) that in Cumae there were still in his time, i.e. about the beginning of our era, many remains of Greek tradition and organization. In Neapolis, he continues (5, 4, 7), despite the necessary cohabitation with the Samnites and Oscans, the Greek kinship groups called *phratríai* and the athletic institutions named *gymnasia* and *ephebeia* still existed. Further, every fourth year a religious festival with contests in sport and musical performances was celebrated in the old Greek manner, and Greek names still occurred together with Campanian ones in the later lists of the city's governors, the so-called *demarchoi*. The Greek way of living found in Neapolis, he continues, enticed many to move there from Rome, drawn by the prospect of a calm and restful old age and of living a relaxed life among like-minded people.

In later times, the Greeks on Capri were of course in lively contact with their kinsmen and the hellenized Campanians in Neapolis, as is evidenced by Neapolitan coins from 380-350 B.C. which have been found on the island. According to Strabo (5, 4, 9), the Neapolitans took possession of Capri, but we do not know when that occurred. It is reasonable, however, to assume that it happened before 326 B.C., when Neapolis fell into the hands of the Romans during the Second Samnite

War. Soon afterwards, Capri too came into contact with the powerful city by the Tiber, as is shown by an item in a collection of hand-written records gathered by the architect A. Carelli and now kept in the archive of the Centro Caprense (IX D, fol. 40). According to this item, some workers in a vineyard at Torre della Guardia near the southwest point of the island in 1923 found a clay jar containing some hundred silver coins from the time of the Roman Republic. Unfortunately, the workers dispersed the majority of the coins, handing over the jar with only twelve coins to the land-owner. These coins were all denarii, showing Victory and a trophy on the reverse, and coined for a short period between 269 and 217 B.C. It is thus clear that Capri during the 3rd century B.C. had trade connections, direct or indirect, with Rome.

The Greeks on Capri probably retained their own inherited traditions and institutions just as long and just as much as the Neapolitans. But we know very little about them. No ancient author found any of the happenings or conditions on the little island worthy of note prior to its becoming imperial property; after that, for instance, Suetonius informs us, in his account of Augustus' visit to the island, that there was, as in Neapolis, an *ephebeion*.

More detailed information on the Greek islanders was no doubt given by the many official and private inscriptions which once must have existed on Capri. But the majority of these inscriptions were destroyed centuries ago by ignorant discoverers, others have been removed from the island and are now difficult to trace, others again have been withheld in private collections too often dispersed. The ninety-seven Latin epitaphs, complete or fragmentary, which are to be seen in Axel Munthe's Villa San Michele, do not allow conclusions about the population of Capri, either in the Greek or in the Roman age, since twentythree of them demonstrably and many more probably come from Rome or other places in Latium or Campania.

The chief epigraphical information about the Greeks on Capri is to be drawn from the 40-odd Greek and Latin inscriptions published in the two corpora entitled Inscriptiones Graecae Italiae et Siciliae (IGI) and Corpus Inscriptionum Latinarum (CIL), as having been found on the island, or referring to persons of Caprean origin. In addition, there are some inscriptions which Norman Douglas and Humbert Kesel have discovered and published. For our purpose it will suffice to quote just a few of these inscriptions which give us insight into the Greek milieu and evidence about the mixture of Greek and Roman elements on Capri.

Three Greek inscriptions concern dedications from persons who had been *agoranómoi,* that is, overseers of the market. One of them (IGI 897a) is a fragment found near the Palazzo a Mare together with a block of granite inscribed with hieroglyphics and fragments of a statue of Isis, or perhaps a priest of Isis. The fragmentary inscription contained a dedication to a freedman of a dead and deified emperor from a person who designates himself as ἀγορανομήσας Καπριήτων, « one who was a market-overseer for the Capreans ». The second inscription (IGI 897) is a fragment found in 1800 near the church of San Nicola at the foot of the « Phoenician Steps »; it contained a dedication from a number of former *agoranómoi* to a living emperor, whose title Kaísar Sebastós (Caesar Augustus) can be reconstructed. The third inscription (IGI 896) mentions an agoranómos named Korinthos Tropianos.

A stone cube found in 1889 near the church of San Costanzo above Marina Grande and now set in a wall in the courtyard of the Casa Rossa in Anacapri bears a Latin inscription consisting of four words: HIPPOD SIMPLEX PASSUS IREREDIRI. The words are probably meant to give information or instruction concerning the length of single and double races taking place in what the Greeks called *hippódromos* and the Romans *circus,* i.e. an enclosure for chariot-racing, which ought to have been situated in the vicinity of where the stone cube was found, the only terrain on the island suitable for such a purpose.

Like everywhere else, the majority of the ancient inscriptions unearthed on Capri are epitaphs. Both the Greek and the Latin ones limit themselves in general to the name of the deceased followed by a more or less stereotyped phrase of farewell or praise. The Latin inscriptions as a rule start with the letters D M, an abbreviation for DIS MANIBUS, the usual formula for the consecration of the deceased to the shades of the dead in the underworld, honoured as divine. A few examples may suffice.

A Greek epitaph (IGI 901), found in 1804 near the ancient lighthouse on Monte Tiberio, says: ΤΑΥΡΙΚΕ ΣΤΑΙΟΥ ΧΑΙΡΕ, « Taurike, Staios' wife, farewell ». A fragmentary epitaph in the Villa Fortino near Palazzo a Mare (IGI 901a) for a wife whose name is not preserved starts with the words ΘΕΟΙΣ ΔΑΙΜΟΣΙ, the Greek equivalent of DIS MANIBUS, and ends with a ΓΛΥΚΥΤΑΤΗ,« the sweetest », and a ΧΑΙΡΕ, « farewell ».

A longer Greek epitaph published by Norman Douglas is said to have been found during Axel Munthe's excavations at Damecuta in 1892 but is no longer at his Villa San Michele. It commemorates a certain Skorpos, saying in one hexameter (not quite free of metrical and orthographic mistakes) and a half pentameter: « In this grave I, Skorpos, repose, comforted by the kind hands of my friends ».

A Latin epitaph (Eph. epigr. No. 672, Add. ad CIL, X) tells about a child's death: EXPECTATUS C. FANNI ANTEROTIS ET FANNIAE SCYNDAE DELICIM (sic) VIXIT ANNOS DVO ET DIES XXXXV, « Expectatus, Caius Fannius Anterotes' and Fannia Skynda's darling, lived two years and 45 days ». The Greek couple Anterotes and Skynda were freed slaves and as usual bore the Roman name of their former master, Caius Fannius; and they gave their little son a Latin name, Expectatus, « Long-desired ».

Two Latin epitaphs from the mainland give us the names of a man and a woman, both of them Greeks from Capri. The one, found at Antium (CIL, I^2, p. 247), says: BATHYLLUS · VER · CAPR · ABYBL, which means that Bathyllus from Capri was a slave in an aristocratic house and was in charge of the library. The other is from Rome (CIL, VI:2, 8958) and commemorates a Dorcas, Julia Augusta's freed slave woman from Capri, who was an *ornatrix,* that is, a helper at her lady's toilette.

A place all of its own among the Greek inscriptions from Capri is held by a marble plaque now preserved in the monastery of the Oratorians in Naples. The plaque is inscribed with an elegiac poem consisting of five hexameters and five pentameters, in which a youth named Hypatos asks the gods of the underworld to accept him in Hades after his *despótes* let him meet a violent death. The inscription must have been found prior to 1741, when it appears with a Latin translation in L.A. Muratori's Novus Thesaurus veterum Inscriptionum, Tomus III. According to G.M. Secondo's Relazione of 1750, the plaque had come to light « a few years earlier » during excavations in the Grotta di Matromania and was handed over to the scholar Matteo Egizio, who translated the inscription into Latin and annotated it. Other annotated Latin translations of the poem were made by A.F. Gori in his Symbolae Litterariae Opuscula, Vol. II, 1752, and by G. Martorelli in his De Regia Theca Calamaria, Vol. II, 1756.

Martorelli translated *despótes* with *Caesar* and thought that Augustus was meant. Later authors, among them Gregorovius, naturally saw the unfortunate Hypatos as one of Tiberius' victims. The Greek word *despótes,* however, has not the meaning of our loan-word « despot », nor is it an imperial title: it simply means one who is master or ruler over another. Thus, the inscription narrates that Hypatos, probably a slave boy, met his death due to the cruelty of his master or, as D.M. Pippidi will have it, of a god, perhaps Mithras. In any case, it can not serve as proof of Tiberius' alleged lust and blood-thirstiness. Its authenticity has been questioned by Norman Douglas among others, who pointed out that Egizio and many other 17th and 18th century scholars were known as forgers of inscriptions.

Undeniably the inscription contains several peculiarities. The ten verses of the poem are nicely aligned, but the letters of the first row are larger than those of the next two rows, which in turn are larger than those of the following seven rows. Even within the same row, the size of the letters varies somewhat. The one who cut the inscription evidently did not calculate the size of the letters according to the space available on each line, and so, though making them smaller and smaller, he had to place the last ones of seven lines under their respective rows. In the first row, he committed an error of so-called haplography, by letting the two final letters of one word also stand for the first two of the next word. For the letter sigma he used the classical form, except in one word, written with the C commonly used during the Empire. To « Hypatos » he accidentally added an O.

These errors, however, are such as would hardly have been committed by a learned forger but very easily by a simple stone cutter who worked mechanically whithout giving much thought to the meaning of the text he was reproducing on the plaque. Thus, the errors speak in favour of the authenticity of the inscription, as well as the fact that the letters are weather-worn.

More notable than Hypatos and other Greeks of Capri was a comic poet who seems to have had success on the mainland during the Hellenistic period, probably during the latter half of the 3rd century B.C. But we know much less about his ability as a poet than we do about the capacity of the anonymous author of poor Hypatos' epitaph. His name is preserved in the item mentioned above from Stephanos' Ethniká, where it is said that Capri was the place where Blaisos, the comic poet, was born. Athenaeus of Naucratis, a scholar of the 2nd century A.D., collecting in his Deipnophista, « The Scholarly

Banquet », a large number of quotes introduced by the learned
diners, has saved the titles of two of Blaisos' works, Saturnos
and Mesotribas, as well as a nice verse from the first of them:

ἑπτὰ μαθαλίδας ἐπίχεε ἁμῖν τῶ γλυκυτάτω.

« Pour us seven goblets full of your sweetest wine! »

IMPERIAL CAPRI

Suetonius tells us (Aug. 92, 2) that when Caesar Octavian saw how an old, withering oak became vigorous again on his arrival at Capreae, he considered it such a positive omen that he acquired the island from the Neapolitans in exchange for Aenaria (Ischia).

According to Dio Cassius (52, 42), the event must have occurred in 29 B.C., when Octavian was on his way back to Rome from Egypt. At that point he had fifteen terrible years behind him. At the age of eigteen he had been informed of the fact that as Gaius Julius Caesar's grand nephew he had been placed in the murdered dictator's will as adoptive son and heir. Thus he entered into a complicated political play in which he made his moves with cold, calculating intelligence and bloody ruthlessness, in conflict with the executor of the will, Caesar's trusted assistant Marc Antony, in alliance with Antony and Lepidus against Caesar's murderers Brutus and Cassius, and once again in conflict with Antony and the Queen of Egypt, Cleopatra: a conflict which ended with the two opponents' defeat in the sea battle at Actium, followed by their suicide and the incorporation of Egypt into the Roman Empire as Ostavian's personal property.

After Lepidus' retirement to private life and Antony's death, Octavian was the sole remaining member of the so-called second triumvirate, the board of three men to whom the Senate and People had transferred absolute power to rule the State. But wisely enough he was careful not to disrupt the republican form of government by making himself a life-time dictator as Julius Caesar did, and equally careful not to defy public opinion by falling for the Egyptian Queen as Antony did, especially since it was being said that she was entertaining the idea of ruling Rome at Antony's or Octavian's side. He handed back to the Senate and the Roman people his far-reaching authority, perhaps already quite conscious of the fact that he was indispensible.

The popular assembly of the city of Rome, its senate, and its magistrates, often hampered by the principle of collegiality, meaning that every magistracy should be filled by at least two officials with equal authority, had for a long time and in many ways shown their inability to rule a world-wide empire, lately by conferring extraordinary power on Pompey for his war against the pirates, and on the members of the second triumvirate. Caesar Octavian changed his triumviral power for another one made up of republican magistratures. As Princeps, the first man in Senate and Empire, invested with the inviolability and full authority of a permanent tribunate, being supreme commander, as Imperator, of all Roman armies and fleets, having proconsular authority over the provinces, and supervising the riches of Egypt, he ruled the vast Empire, under the honorary name of Augustus, so long and so well that his peculiar form of governing became a lasting institution and his name and titles — Caesar, Princeps, Imperator — went to posterity, as Kaiser, Czar, Prince, Emperor.

In becoming imperial property, Capri took a place in world history for some decades. Suetonius says (Aug. 72, 2) that for relaxation, Augustus preferred to retire to the coasts and islands of Campania or to small towns near Rome, such as Lanuvium, Praeneste and Tibur. Strabo's words about his building activity on Capri and Suetonius' information about the fossiles and prehistoric weapons he collected there have already been mentioned. No doubt he visited the island many times, but it is only in Suetonius' account of his last visit (Aug. 98, 1-5) that we find some information of how he spent his time there.

At that time he was almost 76 years old, but nevertheless had decided to accompany his step-son Tiberius on his travel

42

to Illyria, as far as to Beneventum in Campania. Contrary to his custom, he took ship by night from Astura in Latium, skirting the coast of Campania. As he sailed by the bay of Puteoli, it happened that from an Alexandrian ship which had just arrived there, the passengers and crew, clad in white, crowned with wreaths, and burning incense, lavished good wishes and compliments upon him, saying that it was thanks to him that they lived and sailed the seas, thanks to him that they enjoyed freedom and prosperity. This made the Emperor so happy that he gave each of his companions forty gold coins, making them promise on oath to spend the sum only to buy wares from Alexandria.

He then continued his journey to Capri, where he spent four days of rest and recreation in his palace, after an illness he had contracted at sea. On Capri, he showed his generosity by giving his companions various small gifts, and by distributing among them Roman togas and Greek mantles, stipulating that the Romans should dress like Greeks and speak Greek, and the Greeks should wear Roman dress and speak Latin. He continually watched the exercises of the Greek youths, the ephebi, of whom there was still a great number on the island, and he even gave them a dinner at which he himself was also present and not only allowed but insisted that they should freely make jokes and snatch the fruit and delicacies that were being thrown about.

The next section of Suetonius' narration is puzzling and has occasioned many more or less imaginative explanations. In order to give an idea of the difficulties of this passage, the original text, as it has come down to us in the manuscripts, must be quoted: *Vicinam Capreis insulam Apragopolim appellabat a desidia secedentium illuc e comitatu suo. Sed ex dilectis unum, Masgaban nomine, quasi conditorem insulae* κτίστην *vocare consueverat.*

A literal translation of these words would say that Augustus « used to call an island in the vicinity of Capri Apragopolis because of the laziness of some of his companions who

withdrew there. But he used to call one of his favourites,
Masgaba by name, ' Ktistes ', as if he were the founder of the
island ».

The continuation of the narrative causes no problems.
Suetonius gives us a picture of an imperial dinner. He does
not say anything about the menu, but surely it contained fish
and shell fish, both highly prized as delicacies by the Romans.
The coasts of Campania were famous for their fish, and mussels
from Capri were particularly valued, according to Pliny's Naturalis Historia (3, 61 and 30, 45).

Now noticing from his dining-room that a large crowd
with many torches was visiting the tomb of Masgaba, who
had died the year before, Augustus uttered aloud a verse in
Greek, composed offhand:

Κτίστου δὲ τύμβον εἰσορῶ πυρούμενον.
« I see the Founder's tomb alight with fire »

Then turning to Thrasyllos, one of Tiberius' companions
who was reclining opposite him and knew nothing of the matter,
he asked him from what poet he thought the verse was taken.
When Thrasyllos hesitated, Augustus added another Greek
verse:

Ὁρᾶς φάεσσι Μασγάβαν τιμώμενον;
« You see how Masgaba is honoured now whith lights? »

Whereupon he also asked who had composed that line.
When Thrasyllos could say nothing except that the verses were
splendid whoever the author might be, Augustus burst into
a laugh and persevered with his jokes.

Shortly thereafter, continues Suetonius, Augustus crossed
over to Neapolis, although suffering from periodically reoc-
curring stomach pains. In spite of this, he was present at an
athletic contest held every fifth year in his honour, and then
continued his voyage together with Tiberius to Beneventum.
But on the way back, his illness increased and he tock to
his bed in Nola. He called back Tiberius and had a long pri-

vate conversation with him, and after that he did not concern himself with anything of importance. On the last day of his life, he asked his friends whether it seemed to them that he had played his role well in the comedy of life, and added two Greek verses:

'Ἐπεὶ δὲ πάνυ καλῶς πέπαισται, δότε κρότον
καὶ πάντες ἡμᾶς μετὰ χαρᾶς προπέμψατε.

« Since well the play has drawn to a close, all clap your hands, and with your thanks dismiss me from the stage ».

While he was kissing his wife Livia, uttering the words: « Live in the memory of our union, farevell », he met that *euthanasía,* that sudden and painless death which he had always hoped for.

Suetonius' description of Augustus' last visit to Capri gives us many interesting insights into his character and education. He obviously did not belong to those Romans who condescendingly spoke of *Graeculi,* « those little Greeks ». He clearly enjoyed the Greek atmosphere on Capri and frequently visited its *ephebeion,* which probably lay near the imperial palace towards the harbour; and despite his old age and unsteady health, he was always in the mood for joking. With the idea of having his Roman companions pretend to be Greeks and vice versa, he probably wanted to emphasize that all were equal in his eyes. That he could require the Romans to talk Greek and the Greeks Latin, gives evidence of the level of education of his suite. His improvised verses and his witty creation of the word *Apragópolis,* « Lazytown », show that he himself was in complete command of the Greek language and literature.

But what was the « island in the vicinity of Capri » that Augustus used to call Apragopolis? We can safely ignore the fanciful suggestions made by some 18th and 19th century scholars who, unable to detect any other island near Capri, placed Apragopolis on an island which they thought had sunk into the sea after Augustus' time, or on one of the Siren

Islands, which lie about 10 miles (15 km.) from Capri, or else on the island of Nisida, which lies off Pozzuoli, 16 miles (26 km.) from Capri. Quite fanciful is also the idea of D. Romanelli that it lay on Monte Tuoro, which he thought could have been an island which later became a part of Capri due to the earth washed up by the sea.

More sensible is the suggestion made by Feola and Mangoni that Apragopolis could be the rocky islet called Il Monacone, not far from the three Faraglioni near the southeast corner of Capri. This localization seemed to be confirmed by the fact that remains of Roman masonry and a rectangular depression called « Masgaba's tomb » are to be seen on the islet. This depression, however, as stated by Maiuri, is far too big for a grave, and its hard lime-mortar plaster indicates that it was a water cistern or fish tank. Further, the islet is far too small and difficult of access to have been both a holiday paradise and Masgaba's special island, where many people could gather round his tomb. The same objection can be made to Motzo's suggestion that Apragopolis could have been on Punta di Tragara and the landlocked one of the Faraglioni.

Thus, if there is no island in the vicinity of Capri which could have been the site of Apragopolis and Masgaba's tomb, we must assume that Suetonius' words *vicinam Capreis insulam* ought to be understood differently, or else that a copying mistake crept into the text. In his edition of the Lives of the Caesars in the Loeb Classical Library (1919 and 1951), John C. Rolfe took *Capreis* as locative and *vicinam* as partitive, which means that Augustus on Capri called the neighbouring part of the island Apragopolis. This interpretation, however, is very forced and hardly convincing.

The Italian epigrapher Matteo Della Corte held *Capreis* to be a writing-error for *Capreas* and that *insula* here was equivalent to *vicus* or *pagus,* « village », « town », which should mean that Augustus described the nearby town of Capreae, as seen from his palace near the harbour, as Apragopolis. Maiuri, however, has rightly objected to this interpretation, pointing out that *insula,* besides being « an area of land surrounded by water », also means « a collection of houses within four streets », a block, but never a village or a town.

Maiuri himself thought that Augustus, already while he was sailing in with Capri in view, designated the entire island, or a part of it, to wit, Anacapri, as Apragopolis, and that Masgaba's tomb, despite his own observations, was on the Monacone. But this interpretation, requiring the reading *Capreas,* is not satisfying either. The context and the use of imperfect in Suetonius' text shows that Augustus did not hit upon the name Apragopolis during the cruise across the Bay which was to be his last, but had often used it during earlier visits to the island. Masgaba was probably one of Augustus' freedmen, entrusted with the organization and administration of Capri as imperial property, and for that very reason was bestowed by his master with the name of Greek colony-founders, *Ktistes,* « as if he were the founder of the island » — that is, of Capri! It is plausible, therefore, that he had his tomb in one of the normal burial grounds on Capri, not out on some almost inaccessible rock islet.

The meal described by Suetonius was most probably eaten in the palace near the harbour, which is thought to have been Augustus' favourite abode on the island, and whose ruins now are called Palazzo a Mare. Masgaba's tomb probably was on the slope or the terrace above, visible from this palace: that is, in the place where Capri's dead were buried both in the Greek and in the Roman period, and where the town of Capri still has its two cemeteries, one for Catholics, and one for non-Catholic foreigners.

It is possible that Suetonius' statement about Apragopolis originally was clearer than the version given in our codices, for an ancient commentator on one of Juvenal's satires (10, 93-95) says briefly that « Augustus called this island (namely Capri) Apragopolis, because it was a place for indolent people, just as Suetonius says ».

Suetonius tells us (Tib. 21, 2) that when Tiberius had left Augustus after their last confidential talk in Nola, the servants heard the Emperor say to himself: « Alas for the Roman people, to be chewed by such sluggish jaws! » Tiberius was then, in 14 A.D., almost 56 years old. As a child, he had had frightful experiences when his mother Livia and his father, Tiberius Claudius Nero, who had allied himself with Marc Antony, had to flee for their lives from Octavian's troops. He lost his own father at the age of nine, but had then got Augustus as step-father after Livia's marriage to him. He must often have felt that he was caught between a strong-willed mother who wanted to see him succeed Augustus and an all-powerful step-father who openly disliked his closed and stern character. In later years, he had shown great capability in handling military and administrative tasks by the Danube and the Rhine, had celebrated triumphs and had received appreciative words from Augustus. But he had also been subject to many disappointments and humiliations. He had seen himself be passed over when Augustus chose first his nephew Marcellus and, after his death, his friend and helper Marcus Vipsanius Agrippa to be his successor. He had to experience how Augustus adopted and favoured his daughter Julia's and Agrippa's young sons Gaius and Lucius Caesar. He was forced by imperial order to divorce his beloved wife and marry Julia for dynastic reasons after Agrippa's death. Tired of intrigues and Julia's immoral life, he vithdrew for seven years into more or less voluntary exile on Rhodes, where he at last obtained a divorce from Julia.

However, Gaius and Lucius Caesar had both died at an early age, and their younger brother, a ne'er-do-well named Agrippa Postumus, had been banished by Augustus from Rome, just like his mother, Julia, and her daughter, who had her mother's name and character. In the end, Tiberius was the only one of Augustus' family conceivable of being his successor. He received tribunal power and unlimited proconsular authority, and thus was Augustus' co-regent. But, according to Suetonius (Tib. 23), he had also to experience the disgrace of being designated in Augustus' vill as the one the Emperor was forced to choose: « Since a cruel fate has bereft me of my sons Gaius and Lucius, may Tiberius Caesar be the heir to two-thirds of my estate ».

When the time came to take over as Augustus' successor, he refused determinedly, says Suetonius (Tib. 24), and for a long time, to take upon himself a burden that he felt was too heavy for someone of his age. He allowed himself, however, to be persuaded, and from that time on took great pains to be a good and effective administrator like his predecessor.

But rather quickly he must have found his position more and more unbearable. His refusal to succed Augustus, his modesty and his considerateness towards the Senate were interpreted as hypocricy, his disinclination to arrange and be present at gladiatorial games made him unpopular in the eyes of the populace. The situation worsened when his nephew Germanicus, whom he had adopted in 19 A.D. in accordance with Augustus' wishes, died and his vidow, Agrippina, started a hate compaign against the Emperor, blaming him for having caused Germanicus to be poisoned. Tiberius' suspicions against Agrippina were strengthened by Sejanus, the commander of the Pretorian Guard, who had won the Emperor's confidence, especially since he protected him with his own body from rocks falling from the mouth of a cave near Terracina, during his journey to Campania in 26 A.D.

Having traversed Campania, Tiberius went over to Capri and stayed on there, on Sejanus' advice. In the Emperor's absence, Sejanus worked steadily on in Rome for his own advancement. He had complete control over the city, since all the pretorian cohorts were stationed there, and he had taken care that his friends had received important positions in the Empire. He had seduced the wife of the Emperor's son Drusus and counted on becoming her new husband upon the death of Drusus in 23 A.D., caused perhaps by poison. Agrippina and her two eldest sons had been banished, and as conceivable successors to the throne there only remained the Emperor's grandson Tiberius Gemellus and a younger son of Germanicus and Agrippina named Gaius, who from his father's soldiers got the nickname Caligula, « the little soldier boot ». Both of them were far too young to be dangerous for Sejanus.

The conspirator was approaching his goal when information of his intrigues reached Tiberius on Capri, in 31 A.D., through the Emperor's sister-in-law, Antonia. Tiberius was then 73 years old. The counterplot he organized in haste to bring down the traitor gives evidence of his unbroken spirit. But waiting to hear if it succeded or not must have been an almost unbearable strain. Suetonius says (Tib. 65, 2) that he even kept ships in readiness for flight to any of the Empire's legions, constantly watching from a high cliff for the signals that he had arranged to be sent from afar informing of how the events developed, and that even after the conspiracy had been totally crushed, he felt so insecure and anxious that he did not leave the palace called Jupiter's for the next nine months. During that time, a bloody clean-up was taking place. Sejanus, the members of his family and his followers were executed. Agrippina and her two elder sons were starved or starved themselves to death.

After that, Tiberius remained on Capri for good. A summing up of information gathered from Tacitus (Ann. 6, 1; 6, 15; 6, 39), Suetonius (Tib. 72), Dio Cassius (58, 21 and 24) and the Jewish historian Flavius Josephus' history of the Jews (18, 179) shows however that during the years 32-37 he went six times, not just two as Suetonius maintains, to Tusculum or other places near Rome. But he contented himself with seeing his capital from a distance.

On the way back to Capri in 37 he became gravely ill and had to break off his voyage in Misenum, where he was put up in a villa which once belonged to Lucius Lucullus. According to Suetonius (Tib. 68), he had a robust constitution and enjoined excellent health during nearly the whole of his reign, appart from sudden appearances of facial pimples and

50

a few attacks of illness, perhaps more pretended than real; and all this despite the fact that from his thirtieth year he took care of himself without the advice of physicians, whose art, according to Tacitus (Ann. 6, 46), he used to sneer at. But now he was 77 years old and his body, weakened by age, could no longer tolerate the exertions he stubbornly submitted it to. He died March 16th, 37 A.D.

Estimations of Tiberius have gone from one extreme to the other. Velleius Paterculus, who served under Tiberius as officer and official, expresses in his history great admiration for him as military commander, emphasizing his concern for the health of soldiers and officers, but says nothing about any cruelties or acts of violence on his part. Velleius, however, did not live to see Tiberius' last six years after the fall of Sejanus (whom he also admired), and his praise has often been judged as servile ingratiation. Seneca, who as an adult saw the whole of Tiberius' reign, describes (De beneficiis, 3, 26) the terrible denunciations which flourished during these years, without however charging him personally with any vices or excesses. Pliny the Elder, who was 14 years old when Tiberius died, in his Naturalis Historia talks about his *contumeliosus secessus* (7, 149) and says (34, 62) that he was *imperiosus sui inter initia principatus*. But the mention of his « shameful seclusion » on Capri does not allow any conclusion to be drawn about of what the shamefulness consisted. And the other statement is made in connection with the famous story about how Tiberius, « even though he showed self-restraint in the beginning or his rule », could not refrain from having Lysippus' Apoxyomenos, the statue of an athlete scraping himself after a contest, to be moved from its place in front of Agrippa's baths to his own bedroom but had to replace it because of the reaction of the people. With the exception of this implied accusation of inconsiderateness, Pliny has no complaint against Tiberius other than he was very melancholy (28, 23), that he was far from affable (35, 28) and that while young, indulged far too much in wine, while in his old age he was strongly abstemious (14, 144).

51

Suetonius of course (Tib. 42) has also quite a bit to say about Tiberius' drinking habits.

It was not until long after Tiberius' death that Tacitus, Suetonius and Dio Cassius created the repugnant picture of the Emperor which was reproduced by so many later authors: the picture of a man who for a long time knew to hide his true character but once he came into power allowed his blood-thirstiness and debauchery to come forth, above all in the notorious death sentences for crimes against the state and the equally notorious excesses he delighted in on Capri. In order to explain this picture, certain modern authors have gathered such items from the three ancient defamers' works as seemed to indicate that Tiberius suffered from Caesarean madness, persecution mania or a schizophrenic psychosis ending in a senile dementia which manifested itself, on Capri, in sadistic and sexual excesses.

A careful and critical examination of the historical sources, however, has resulted in a more fair and varied judgement. It has been pointed out, among other things, that the treason trials, in which the Senate was the sentencing authority, were not conceived by Tiberius, that he intervened more than once to reduce a sentence, and that he, prior to Sejanus' treachery, only in one case approved a death sentence. One of the many who were accused as being friends of Sejanus defended himself frankly, saying that one of those friends had been no other than the Emperor himself — and was acquitted. It has also been convincingly shown by the Swedish psychiatrist Sven Hedenberg that the claims for Tiberius' mental illness are based on very weak and ambiguous grounds; and these claims have also been refuted by the German medical historian Albert Esser.

But it seems quite natural that Tiberius, being of a melancholic disposition, obedient to duty, and contempting display and popularity, because of the many insults, misfortunes and disappointments he experienced became more and more bitter and suspicious, more and more misanthropic, more and more ruthless in preserving his own safety, and more and more cautious and slow in his actions. How he viewed his situation in the hostile world he had to govern is revealed by his saying, quoted by Suetonius (Tib. 25, 1), that he was holding a wolf by the ears.

Naturally there was a lot of speculation about what led Tiberius to his surprising decision to abandon his capital and take up residence on the little island in the Bay of Naples. Suetonius says (Tib. 40) that Tiberius was particularly attracted to that island because it was accessible by only one small beach, being everywhere else girt with sheer cliffs of great height and by deep water. Tacitus (Ann. 4, 67) describes the favourable climate of the island and the view of what was « the most beautiful bay before the eruption of Vesuvius changed the appearance of the landscape »; but he emphasizes that above all else, Tiberius probably appreciated the isolation and difficult access of the island, which prevented anyone from landing there unseen. He also writes, however (Ann. 4, 41 and 57), that he has followed earlier authors who said that Tiberius retired to Capri because of Sejanus' intrigues, but since the Emperor remained on the island six years after the latter's downfall, he is uncertain of what was the real reason: perhaps it was more likely that he did it to keep his cruelty and vices secret (as Suetonius means, Tib. 42, 1) or, according to what some thought, because he was ashamed of his thin and stooped body, his bald pate and his facial pimples, or even, as others suggested, because he wanted to get away from his mother Livia's ascendancy.

These explanations, however, are mere guesses, rather naive and more or less biased by the desire to interpret everything for the worst. Livia died in 29 A.D., that is, only three years after Tiberius had moved to Capri. That he could hide any excesses or physical flaws by moving there is totally unrealistic. His habits and appearance must have been well known to the local inhabitants and to the many officials, secretaries, servants, workers, officers and soldiers necessary for administration, service, guard-duty, and the building and maintenance of edifices on the Emperor's island. In addition to all these, there were missions from different parts of the Empire and those who came to Capri with communiqués from the Senate in Rome, and who often seem to have had to wait a long time for the Emperor's reply. We know that Tiberius also had many guests who stayed with him for some time and certainly would not have appreciated orgies, among them the famous jurist Cocceius Nerva and the knight Curtius Rufus, plus a number of literati, mainly Greeks, whose conversation was highly valued by the Emperor, according to Tacitus (Ann. 4, 57). There were also Sejanus and his successor Macro, who had an important role in crushing the traiter's plot; further, the young Tiberius Gemellus, the young Vitellius, who is described by Suetonius (Vit. 3, 2) as one of Tiberius' « pleasure boys », and who at a mature age posed for some months as the successor of Nero. And there was the young Gaius Caligula, who according to the same author (Cal. 10-11) was so forgetful of the fate of his kindred, so insensitive to what he himself had to bear, so obsequious towards the Emperor and so willing to participate in his excesses that it was well said of him that no one had ever been a better slave or a worse master. Later on, says Suetonius (Cal. 12, 3), Caligula was said to have admitted, certainly not having killed Tiberius, but having planned to do so: for he boasted constantly that he had once entered the bedchamber of the sleeping Emperor dagger in hand, to revenge the death of his mother and brothers, but that, seized with pity, he had flung down the dagger and gone out again; and that Tiberius, though he found out about the incident, never dared do anything to him, Gaius. The story is too boastful to be true.

Another of Tiberius' guests on Capri was Marcus Julius Agrippa, whose hazardous life is described by Josephus in his History of the Jews (Books 18-19) and his History of the Jewish War (Book 2). This Agrippa was the grandson of the King of the Jews Herod I, known from the Bible for his

slaughter of the children of Bethlehem and from history as an
energetic and ruthless tyrant who was clever enough to keep
in with the Romans. Julius Agrippa was taken as a youth to
Rome by his mother Berenice to avoid the fate of his father,
his uncles, his grandmother and other relatives, who were executed by his terrible grandfather Herod. Being members of
a royal family, and granted Roman citizenship, mother and
son were taken into the imperial family, and the boy was
raised together with the princes. After Berenice's death he led
the gay life of the spendthrift in Rome together with Tiberius'
son Drusus and other companions of the same sort. Then Drusus
died too, and Agrippa left Rome and a large amount of unpaid
debts, including one to the imperial treasury. He went to Palestine where, after various entanglements with relatives and
the Roman governor, he secured a loan at a usurious rate of
interest. He then proceeded to Alexandria, where he got a new
loan which enabled him to return to Italy. From Puteoli he
boldly crossed over to Capri to pay his respects to Tiberius.
The Emperor welcomed him courteously, but being informed
of his enterprises already the next day, he refused to see him
until he had paid off his debts. The debtor was saved from
disgrace by his faithful protectoress Antonia, Tiberius' sister-
in-law, who advanced him the sum he owed the imperial treasury. The Emperor once again was gracious and asked Agrippa
to take up with the young Tiberius Gemellus when in Rome.
Once there our adventurer obtained a large loan from a Sa-
maritan, paid back his debt to Antonia and had a lot of
money over. But he deemed it more advantageous for the
future to keep in with Gaius Caligula than with Tiberius Gemellus, and future events proved him right. Things looked dark
for him, however, when it reached Tiberius' ears that during
a ride with Gaius, he had said that he prayed to God that
Tiberius might soon depart this life and leave the rule to Gaius
who in all respects was more worthy. He was duly put into
prison, and when there, a fellow inmate interpreted the appearance of an owl as a sign that he would die within five

days if he saw that bird again. But before anything worse happened to him, Tiberius passed away. Gaius became Emperor, put Tiberius Gemellus to death, and rewarded his friend Agrippa with three tetrarchies in Palestine. Gaius himself was murdered after less than four years of rule, but Agrippa made sure to keep in good standing with his successor Claudius, who made him king of Judaea. As Herod Agrippa, the adventurer proved to be a good regent, had the confidence of the Romans, observed the Ten Commandments in the cities of the Jews, and was a broad-minded man-of-the-world outside of them. But, says Josephus, when he one day sat upon his throne in splendid glittering attire and permitted the people to praise him like a god without contradiction, he caught sight of an owl, felt a sharp pain in his gut and died five days later. In the Acts of the Apostles (ch. 12) his miserable end is described as a punishment from the Lord: he had ordered the Apostle Jacob to be beheaded and thrown Peter into prison to please the Jews, and when he sat attired in kingly robes and un-protestingly heard the people praise his words like the voice of God, the angle of the Lord smote him and he was eaten up by worms and gave up his ghost.

The motley crowd which surrounded Tiberius on Capri was of course the major source of those rumors about his terrible excesses which Suetonius describes (Tib. 43-44): how he invented so-called *sellaria,* which ought to mean « rooms with chairs », in which groups of young girls, debauched men and inventors of unnatural forms of sexual intercourse, which he called *spintriae,* engaged in fornication three by three in front of the Emperor to stimulate his waning desire; how he had his bedrooms decorated with the most indecent paintings and sculptures and furnished with the lascivious books of the Greek authoress Elephantis; how he had youths and girls, dressed up like fauns and nymphs, to prostitute themselves in caves and recesses in the rocks; and how he devoted himself to even worse debaucheries of a kind, according to Suetonius, that

one hardly should tell about or hear told, to say nothing of
believing — and which he then proceeds to relate in detail.

Suetonius has a lot to narrate as well about Tiberius'
sadistic cruelty (Tib. 69): how, shortly after his arrival on
Capri, when a fisherman came up unexpectedly and offered
him a huge mullet, he was so alarmed by the man's having
climbed up over rough and pathless rocks from the back of
the island that he had his face scrubbed with the fish; and
when the fisherman praised his luck for not having offered a
large crab which he had caught, he had his face lacerated with
the crab also; how he had one of his body guards executed
for stealing a peacock from his preserves; and how he had
a centurion whipped half to death because he had not cleared
the way when the Emperor's sedan chair got entangled in the
shrubs. Suetonius also tells us (Tib. 62, 2) that on Capri people
still pointed out the place where Tiberius had his tortured
victims cast headlong into the sea, while marines waited below
for the bodies and broke their bones with oars and boat hooks
to insure that no one survived. Further, says Suetonius, Tiberius had devised a special form of torture in which the victim
was tricked into drinking much wine and then tied up in
such a way that he was unable to urinate.

Most of these and other tales of Tiberius' terrible excesses
cannot claim absolute credibility. They originate from gossip
which no doubt, like most juicy anecdotes throughout the ages,
was repeated in more and more « improved » form and set
on paper only fifty years or more after Tiberius' death, primarily by Suetonius, who busily gathered and uncritically retold
all sorts of scandals in his Lives of the Caesars. It is however
worthwhile to note that Suetonius himself admits that the foul-
est of the sexual orgies ascribed to Tiberius can not be considered credible. The tale of how Tiberius had his victims
thrown into the sea does not seem quite convincing either,
since no cliff on Capri is so absolutely vertical that someone
could be hurled off the top directly into the water, necessitating
clubbing him to death with oars and boat hooks.

On the other hand, it is surely going too far to the other extreme when the English historian M. Cary claims that everything that was told about Tiberius' cruelties and perversions on Capri is no more to be believed than if similar things were said about old Queen Victoria of England. It is natural that during the eleven years he lived on Capri as a disappointed, suspicious and misanthropic old man, Tiberius was quick to smell treachery and insubordination around him and had no qualms about using severe punishment as a deterrent. The stories about his sedan chair getting caught in the shrubs and the fisherman popping up from an unexpected direction cannot be rejected as being untrue: his reaction in both cases is psychologically explainable, as is his scant appreciation of the fisherman's gallows humor. The accounts of Tiberius' sexual orgies on Capri are probably not complete fabrications either, although enormously exaggerated. Perhaps the old Emperor, like many other elderly people, stimulated his dying sexual desire with erotic pictures and *tableaux vivants,* probably no more arousing than the pornography which shrewd film producers, photographers and writers hand out nowadays to the whole world. A marble well-mouth from Capri, now in the British Museum (Fig. 16), may illustrate with its erotic relief groups the kind of sculpture that Tiberius loved to erect in his palaces on the island.

In addition to what the administration of the great empire and the little island required, Tiberius seems to have been engaged on Capri in writing the memoirs and transactions that according to Suetonius (Dom. 20) constituted Domitian's only reading, and the loss of which must be regretted for more than one reason. According to the same author (Tib. 70), he also wrote poems in Latin and Greek, and was particularly interested in mythology. He often amused himself by asking scholars posers, such as « Who was Hecuba's mother? », « What was the name of Achilles when dressed like a girl among the princesses on Scyrus? », or « What did the Sirens usually sing? »

But what seems to have occupied him more than anything else was his old mania, shared with many, of reading the future with the help of astrological observations and calculations. Tacitus reports (Ann. 6, 20-21) how he was initiated into the art by the astrologer Thrasyllos on Rhodes. He used to order one of his freedmen, a big and strong fellow, to take any astrologer whose art of prediction he wished to test up to his palace on the cliffs along steep and difficult paths, and upon the slightest suspicion of incompetence or dishonesty on the part of the fortune-teller, he would have the freedman fling him into the sea on the return way. Among those whom Tiberius wished to test in this way was also Thrasyllos. He made an impression on the inquirer by predicting that he was destined to rule the Empire; but then he was asked if he had cast his own horoscope and knew how the year and the day would end for him. The poor astrologer studied the position of the stars and answered, trembling for fear of ending up like many of his colleagues, that he was threatened by mortal danger. Upon hearing this, Tiberius hugged him and wished him luck and awarded him his full confidence. The story is good but would have fit in better among those which were told about Tiberius' life on Capri, where Thrasyllos belonged to his closest circle (cf. above, p. 44).

According to what Josephus reports in his History of the Jews (18, 8-9), Tiberius' superstitious belief in signs and omens influenced even his choice of a successor. In trying to choose between his grandson Tiberius Gemellus and his brother's grandson Gaius Caligula, both equally unsuited in his opinion, he asked the gods on his deathbed to have the one they chose enter his room first, as a sign, — and then asked Gemellus' teacher to send his pupil to him as fast as possible. But Caligula got there first, and Tiberius with heavy heart and warning words left the Roman Empire in his hands.

There were naturally many rumors circulating about Tiberius' death. Some believed, according to Suetonius (Tib. 73, 2; Cal. 12, 2), that Gaius gave him a slow-acting poison, others that one refused to give him food, still others that he was suffocated with a pillow or that Gaius, after having tried in vain to pull off his ring, had a pillow thrown over him and then strangled him with his bare hands. Dio Cassius (58, 28) has a similar account of Gaius' and Macro's actions at the deathbed. Tacitus narrates (Ann. 6, 50) how Caligula, believing Tiberius' death a *fait accompli,* was already celebrating his succession when word arrived that Tiberius had revived and sent for food, upon which Macro put an end to the confusion by suffocating the Emperor under a pile of bedclothes. But Suetonius also refers to the testimony given by Seneca, saying that Tiberius, when he felt death approaching, took off his ring to pass it to someone but then placed it back on his own finger, rang for the servants and, when no one came, got up but then fell dead by the side of the bed.

Of all these different versions of Tiberius' demise, the one given by his contemporary Seneca seems to be the most probable: that Tiberius, weakened by age and the exertions he exposed himself to on the return voyage to Capri, defied his illness to the end and died a natural death. What Suetonius, Tacitus and Dio Cassius report later on about his being poisoned, starved to death or suffocated belongs to the growth of rumors which flourished so abundantly around this Emperor.

Once Capri was converted to imperial property, according to Strabo (5, 4, 9), Augustus started erecting buildings on the island. What was built for the Emperor's needs was obviously one or several edifices of the type defined by the Romans as a *villa,* that is, a more or less palatial dwelling, especially in the country, with a greater or lesser number of rooms and halls, corridors and porticos, and with spacious parks and gardens. Roman senators, generals and other important men during the last hundred years of the Republic usually had several such villas, in the Alban Hills, in Tibur (now Tivoli), by the coasts of Latium and Campania, and in many other places in Italy.

In Rome Augustus lived in a small house on the Palatine, which according to Suetonius (Aug. 73) caused surprise in later days due to its simple furnishing. It was reverently spared when later Emperors erected their palaces close to it and is shown even today, as « Livia's House ». But when he went on vacation with a large suite of friends, servants and body guards, he naturally needed the larger space and resources of a Roman villa.

What has been said about Augustus' needs is of course valid, and to an even greater extent, as regards Tiberius, who lived on Capri almost continuously for eleven years. We don't know, however, how many villas he inherited from Augustus and how many were built by himself. According to Tacitus, all together there were no less than twelve. Tacitus presents this information in a couple of sentences (Ann. 4, 67) which are typical of the author's verbal artistry, and in connection with a remark in Suetonius (Tib. 65, 2) have caused much discussion.

According to the codices, Tacitus says: *Graecos ea tenuisse Capreasque Telebois habitatas fama tradit. Sed tum Tiberius duodecim villarum nominibus et molibus insederat.* Two sentences tersely alluding to a long course of events of immeasurable historical importance: « According to tradition Greeks once ruled these territories and Capreae was inhabited by Teleboans. But now Tiberius had settled there among the names and mighty walls of his twelve villas ».

Suetonius, according to some of the best codices, gives the following piece of information (Tib. 65, 2): *Verum et oppressa coniuratione Seiani nihilo securior aut constantior per novem proximos menses non egressus est villa, quae vocatur Ionis.* This would mean that Tiberius, « even after he had crushed Sejanus' conspiracy, he was in no way more secure and calm, and during the succeeding nine months did not leave the villa which is called Io's. One of the older codices, however, and many of the later onces, instead of *Ionis* offer the reading *Iovis.*

These two passages may be combined into a meaningful statement only by assuming, as did many philologists of old, that *Iovis* is the correct reading in Suetonius, *Ionis* an old copying error, and by considering, as did Maiuri, that *nominibus* in Tacitus is a copying mistake for *numinibus*. This makes Tacitus' remark much more significant, meaning that Tiberius settled « among the gods and mighty walls of his twelve villas », while Suetonius says that he closed himself into « that villa which is called Jupiter's ». And from this we may conclude that the twelve imperial villas on Capri bore the names of the twelve great Olympian gods, and that the most impressive of these villas was named after the supreme god, Jupiter.

H. Kesel, it is true, putting too much trust on the care and judgment of the antique and medieval copyists, agreed with M. Ihm and others who asserted that the villa in question was named after Io, the Argive princess who was changed into a cow guarded by the all-seeing Argos, and that Tacitus by *nominibus* only meant to say that the imperial villas on Capri had different names. It seems unlikely, however, that the subtle stylist Tacitus wished only to communicate such banal information, or that he could expect that his readers would understand that he was talking about special names suitable for the mighty walls of the twelve villas, to wit: names of gods. The arguments advanced in support of the reading *Ionis,* moreover, are very weak: that in « Livia's House » in Rome, there is a painting of Io guarded by Argos, and that therefore there was perhaps a similar painting in the villa on Capri which motivated the naming; that the myth of Io may have been brought from its native island of Euboea to Capri by Greek colonists; and that Tiberius, according to Suetonius (Tib. 69), believed less in the gods than in astrological calculations and omnipotent fate — but with his interest in mythology it would have been quite natural for him to name his villas after the great gods.

We know nothing about the fate of these villas after Tiberius' death, with the exception of one of them which was abandoned after the eruption of Vesuvius in 79 A.D. (see below, p. 79 f.). Some of them seem to have been maintained over a longer period of time, to judge from a remark by G.M. Secondo saying that shortly before 1750, a lead water pipe bearing the name of Marc Aurelius was found on the island. He and other emperors and members of their families probably stayed on Capri for shorter periods. But we know of only one such visit, and that was a compulsory and tragic one. Dio Cassius relates (73, 4, 6) that Commodus (180-193), Marc Aurelius' degenerate son, had his sister Lucilla and his unfaithful wife Crispina sent to Capri as prisoners after their abortive conspiracy against his life. According to Dio, both of them were later executed there, while Commodus' biographer Lampridius states (5, 7) that only Lucilla came to that awful end.

The imperial villas on Capri were of course adorned in the manner that both noble and less distinguished people considered a regular standard of living ever since the time of the later Republic: wall paintings and stucco reliefs, floors covered with mosaics or variegated marble slabs laid in geometric patterns (so-called *sectilia pavimenta*), bronze and marble sculptures, central heating for the rooms and baths by the *hypocaust* system, with warm air circulating in the walls and under the floors. But all such things, which in Pompeii, Herculaneum and Stabiae were protected under thick layers of volcanic ash, in Ostia under sand dunes, and in Rome under vast imperial palaces, have in Capri, as in most other places in the ancient world, been subject throughout the entire middle ages to continuous destruction at the hand of people who took building materials from the ruins, burnt lime from the marble, melted down bronze objects and torn down walls to enlarge their farming areas. This devastation continued even during the Renaissance, in spite of its great admiration of classical art, which gave rise to an interest for saving and collecting at least such ancient bronze and marble sculptures that were tolerably well preserved. In the 18th century again, when the discovery of the three buried towns in Campania aroused a new great interest in classic art, this led also to a ruthless plundering of their buildings which were stripped of their wall paintings, mosaics, sculptures, and other ornaments.

Ever since the imperial villas on Capri were abandoned, which probably occurred, at the latest, after an earthquake in 366, they have been exposed to destruction as mentioned, through which their ruins have been greatly reduced and in many cases completely or almost completely destroyed. The only things that were preserved were whole or nearly whole columns and capitals which could be used as supports primarily in churches, as well as floors and statues which could decorate palaces and museums.

The earliest reports of finds of this type are to be found in the Jesuit Nicolao Parthenio Giannettasio's Autumni Surrentini, of 1698, and in Domenico-Antonio Parrino's Di Capri, il Seno Cratere, of 1700. The latter relates how one « recently » found statues and a beautiful marble floor at the church of Santa Maria di Cetrella, the former describes an almost uninjured marble statue which was found among the ruins of Tiberius' palace on the high north-east corner of the island.

This palace, which in the 18th century was generally identified as the Villa Jovis, very soon became an object of interest for treasure hunters. G.M. Secondo mentions in his Relazione of 1750 how some years earlier one found a floor of variegated marble slabs there, which was broken up and laid out in the church of Santo Stefano, where it can be seen today in front of the high altar (Fig. 9). In the same palace were also found, in addition to a marble statue of a nymph, some pieces of columns of giallo antico, which were used for decoration of the altar in Santo Stefano and San Salvatore, as well as a number of sapphires and garnets which now decorate the image of San Costanzo, the patron saint of the island.

At some time most likely in the 1770's, a relief representing the oriental god Mithras sacrificing a bull (Fig. 19) was found on Capri, according to Rezzonico, near the Grotta di Matromania, according to others, at San Costanzo. The relief was presented by Dr. Gennaro Arcucci to Ferdinand IV and is now in the Museo Archeologico Nazionale in Naples. It has been confused in the Museum, and by more than one author, with a similar but more clumsy relief from Posillipo which according to its inscription was dedicated OMNIPOTENTI DEO MITHRAE by a certain APPIUS CLAUDIUS FARRONIUS DEXTER. The Capri relief, whose figures are illustrated in Romanelli's edition of Rezzonico's and other authors' works, is not a master piece either but important as proof that Mithras had its proselytes even on this island.

In the 1770's a prominent botanist, Dr. Luigi Giraldi from Ferrara, stayed a while on the island. He acquired a fine collection of antiquities by digging in various ruins and bying what peasants happened to find. Giraldi was also working on a book about Capri for which the engraver G. Volpato made a plate or, as was also said, no less than fifty plates. The book was never printed, and Giraldi's collection and Volpato's plates have been sought after in vain by Norman Douglas. The loss of the collection is regrettable, but even more so is the disappearance of the plates, if they really were fifty in number, because most of the Roman ruins that 18th century artists saw on Capri are today still more reduced or completely destroyed.

The major cause of this destruction was the extensive plundering of the ruins performed, a few years after Giraldi's visit, by Norbert Hadrawa. This Hadrawa was an official attached to the Austrian embassy at Ferdinand IV's court in Naples. In 1786 he was given the honour of accompanying the King's hunting expedition to Capri. While the Bourbon ruler and his courtiers hunted quail and pretty girls, Hadrawa got the idea of asking permission to hunt antiquities on the island. This was graciously permitted, on the condition that the King got his share of the booty. Whereupon Hadrawa engaged upon despoiling the ruins through a series of diggings which he describes in a number of letters to a friend in Vienna. In these letters, which came out in print both in Italian and in German, he narrates his exploits with naive complacency: how in a villa on the north slope of Castiglione he dug out four rooms and a bath and in one of the rooms found a floor of variegated marble slabs which were broken up and shipped to the royal museum in Naples, while a sculptured marble vase, two children's heads of marble and a fragment of an archaistic marble relief showing Apollo and Nike were sold to foreign buyers; how he dug in the large area of ruins west of Marina Grande which is called Palazzo a Mare, from where he had two similar marble floors and columns of cipollino carted off, together with 900 cantari white and 700 cantari variegated marble fragments, which together probably equal about 88 tons of marble; how he acquired a cylindrical marble altar decorated with a ram's head bearing garlands which had been unearthed earlier in the same place, and which he is said to have sold to the British Ambassador Sir William Hamilton in Naples who is incorrectly said to have donated it to the British Museum; and how in 1793 he excavated several rooms in the Villa Jovis but due to opposition from the priests at the chapel of Santa Maria del Soccorso which is situated near the ruins was forced to stop his activities there. Praise be to the priests for that! Instead, in 1804 he dug at the adjacent antique lighthouse and found there among other things a terracotta relief with two female figures, capriciously identified as portraits of Crispina and Lucilla, as well as a grave relief with three figures and the Greek inscription mentioned above to the memory of Taurike, wife of Staio.

Hadrawa combined his diplomatic activity with the search and sale of antiquities in the unembarrassed manner of the time, causing irreparable damage to our knowledge of the ancient monuments of Capri. The plundered ruins were left to crumble away or to be further destroyed by farmers' hoes or by the

English and French fortifications in the beginning of the 19th century. The discovered objets d'art were sold mainly to foreign buyers and it is difficult or impossible now to trace and identify them. A few objects were incorporated into Sir William Hamilton's impressive collection of antiques which ultimately was acquired by the British Museum. This museum now owns three marble sculptures from Capri: an altar decorated with reliefs and sphinxes (Fig. 17), donated by Sir William in 1772; the well-mouth mentioned above, with erotic scenes in relief (Fig. 16), also acquired in 1772; and a marble bust of a man engaged in a sacrifice, with his toga drawn up over his head (Fig. 13), bought in 1878 and formerly considered to be a portrait of Tiberius, though it has no similarity to his well-known features. It is to be noted, however, that none of these sculptures originate from Hadrawa's excavations, as in shown by the dates of acquisition.

Hadrawa's descriptions of the devastation caused by himself are valuable through the information he gives on ruins now vanished and through the engravings, some of them coloured, which illustrate several of his most important finds. It is regrettable, therefore, that the planned second volume of his letters was never published after his death in 1810 and that his manuscript and illustrations for it seem to have been lost. Count C. della Torre Rezzonico's Descrizione dell'Isola di Capri, published by D. Romanelli, gives scant consolation for the loss, and the same may be said of C.J. Stegmann's Fragmente über Italien, published anonymously in 1798, being a collection of diary notes including information about the antiquities Hadrawa had in 1797 and his prices. It is also lamentable that so much of other old records about and drawings of Capri's ancient monuments has been dispersed and destroyed through ignorance and indifference, and that Alvino's and Quaranta's large-scale work on Capri's ruins had to be left incomplete.

In 1827 Giuseppe Feola, then mayor of Capri, undertook a limited excavation in the Villa Jovis and brought to light two well-mouths of marble decorated with acanthus leaves and grape vines in relief (Fig. 15) and a fine marble relief showing a young man and a girl on a horse being led by a youth towards a country shrine indicated by a tree and a statue on a column hung with a garland (Fig. 18). This idyllic scene was of course interpreted as a representation of Tiberius and his lover! These sculptures are now in the Museo Archeologico Nazionale in Naples.

On his death Feola left a great amount of manuscripts with notes on discoveries and monuments on Capri, which according to Norman Douglas ended up as wrapping paper at grocery and tobacco shops. There is still, however, a lot of them preserved in the library of the Centro Caprense, including a Rapporto dello stato dell'Isola di Capri al Colonnello Alvarez y Lobo del 28 Novembre 1828, as well as his Rapporto sullo stato attuale dei ruderi Augusto Tiberiani nell'Isola di Capri, of 1830, which more than sixty years later was published by Ignazio Cerio. A more detailed description of the same kind, built to a large extent on Feola's observations, is R. Mangoni's Ricerche topografiche ed archeologiche sull'Isola di Capri, printed in 1834. In addition to the Villa Jovis with the ancient lighthouse, Palazzo a Mare with the ruins called Bagni di Tiberio and the villa on Castiglione partially excavated by Hadrawa, and where, according to I. Cerio, several other rooms with wall paintings and mosaic and marble floors were uncovered in 1857, Feola and Mangoni describe a series of Roman ruins which existed on various sites but are now mostly destroyed, hidden under buildings and gardens or for one reason or another inaccessible.

Among the latter are the ruins on Monte San Michele, whose top according to Weichardt was enlarged by means of mighty foundation walls of Roman concrete, so as to form a square base for a building whose remains were destroyed when the English during the Napoleonic Wars built a fort there. Below it, the hill was encircled by a 39-foot (12 meter) wide terrace with a row of arched rooms on the outer side, connected by doors: a construction which Weichardt thought to have been the substruction for a street or a racing ground. The ascent to the hill was indicated by an arched gate. A vaulted cistern on the north side was changed in early Christian times into a chapel dedicated to the Archangel Michael — not to be confused with the 14th century church of San Michele, or della Croce, on the south side of the hill. Unfortunately what remains of these constructions has been left to disintegrate without ever having been the object of a scientific excavation because the hill has been inaccessible ever since it was purchased by the English family Portland, who changed the area into a fancy garden. Since the rectangular plateau on the top of the hill seemed unsuitable for an imperial villa and a broken circular base found on the spot was thought to have carried a column whose estimated height of 26 feet (8 meters) seemed too much for the storeys of such a villa, Weichardt guessed that Monte San Michele had once been crowned by a temple — a hypothesis represented as a fact by Trower and Kesel! The hypothesis is attractive, but a thorough archaeological investigation of all the ruins on the hill is necessary to prove or disprove it.

Near Punta Tragara south of Monte Tuoro ruins of a Roman villa were brought to light in 1880. Many of its rooms with wall paintings and mosaic and marble floors were unearthed, and one of the latter was taken up and placed in the Cappella del Rosario in the church of Santo Stefano, where it still is today. There were also found some large roofing tiles with stamps reading YACINTHI IULIAE AUGUSTAE; the manufacturer Hyacinthus probably was one of Empress Livia's freedmen. Below this villa, in the little bay called Porto di Tragara, there are remains, under the water, of a small Roman harbour.

Tiles with the same stamp were discovered already in 1826 during the excavation of a villa west of Monte Tuoro, above the rocky islet called Scoglio dell'Unghia Marina, south of the Certosa, the Carthusian monastery. Here, too, was discovered a floor of variegated marble slabs which was taken to the Royal Museum in Naples. It is possible that the monastery itself was also built on remains of Roman constructions, to judge from certain reports about marble fragments and coins found there.

Remains of Roman masonry in *opus reticulatum* prove that the castle on the top of the Castiglione hill was also constructed on the ruins of a Roman building. Other remains of Roman masonry near Scoglio delle Sirene are probably what is left of a mooring place for boats.

Along the street in the town of Capri which leads towards Punta Tragara, instead of the present-day row of shops one saw in olden times a series of uniform arched rooms which gave the street its name, Via Camerelle. The alleged discovery in this place of antique medallions with various scenes of sexual intercourse, the so-called *nummi spintrii,* led Norbert Hadrawa and D. Romanelli to identify these archways as Tiberius' *sellaria*: a ridiculous idea perpetuated for a long time. Actually these vaulted rooms, as was already realized by Feola, served as water reservoirs and substructions for an ancient road which led to the imperial villa near Punta Tragara.

On the slope down towards Marina Grande there were many other Roman water cisterns which are now destroyed or built over. The great number of such cisterns is due to the fact that this slope, and the corresponding one down towards Cala di Mulo, are the only places on Capri where the rain water welled forth from the earth in spings (Truglio near Marina Grande, Acquaviva and Marroncella higher up) thanks to the impermeable tufa bedrock, whereas the rain water everywhere else on the island disappears into the porous limestone rock. Mangoni counts eleven cisterns which provided the Roman villas in the area with water, and which with the passage of time became filled with fine mud. In one of them were found, shortly before 1750, the head and part of the shoulders of an Egyptian porphyry statue which, unfortunately, seems to be lost. In a vineyard near Truglio, owned by Dr. Gennaro

70

Arcucci, a marble statue of a toga-clad Roman somewhat above life-size was found in Hadrawa's time and sent to Rome, where its lost head was replaced by an ancient portrait head of Tiberius. This statue was acquired by the Vatican but was later included in the vast amount of ancient sculpture that Napoleon removed to his museum in Paris, and since it happened not to be among those items which were returned after his fall, it now belongs to the Musée du Louvre (Fig. 11).

Excavations carried out near Truglio during Francis I's reign (1825-1830) also brought to light the remains of several rooms of a Roman villa, with mosaic floors, and five marble statues, all without heads. One of these statues was much above life-size and, therefore, was thought to represent Tiberius, while another one, smaller, is said to have represented a young warrior. These two statues were sent to the Royal Museum in Naples, while a third figure with a bouquet in its hand was sold by the landowner to an Englishman. The fourth and fifth were so badly broken that they were left where they were found, which was unfortunate since one of them bore the signature of the sculptor: IVLIVS SALIVS FECIT.

In a place called Villanova, to the east of Truglio, other ruins with marble floors were uncovered at about the same time, and there, too, a marble statue was found. This was never described in detail and has disappeared, we do not know how.

Yet another Roman villa lay on the rise above the church of San Costanzo. From this villa, according to D. Romanelli, came the eight columns, four of cipollino and four of giallo antico, which supported the cupola and the vaults in this church. They served in this capacity until 1755, when the four giallo antico columns were sent by royal decree to Caserta where they were sawed up and used to decorate the chapel of the castle. A fifth column was sawed into pieces and used to ornament the altar in the church of Santo Stefano in Capri. As late as the beginning of the 19th century, Romanelli saw lead water pipes and several variegated marble floors belonging to this villa, whose remains today are completely destroyed or covered over.

Other similar remains were found nearby in the direction of the sea, in a place called Campo Pisco, i.e. *Campus Episcopi,* since a bishop, Gallo by name, laid out fields for planting there. Here was found, among other things, a bust of Vesta, the later fate of which is unknown.

A considerable number of Roman villas lay also on the Anacapri side of the island. Feola reports that « many years earlier », that is, prior to 1830, when some houses were built in the area called Capodimonte, close to where the « Phoenician Steps » lead up to the medieval gate of Anacapri (Fig. 4), there were unearthed remains of ancient walls and mosaic and marble floors, and that in the same place about 1830 similar remains were brought to light during diggings for the enlargement of a garden belonging to a Count Gallo from Naples. Feola's report is supplemented by his contemporary Mangoni, who describes the discovery in the same area of extensive Roman walls, the remains of a series of rooms all equal in size, bases, capitals and broken columns, fragments of statues, and a little dog in marble. But all this, says Mangoni, was covered up again for the planting of grapevines, so that only a few remnants of walls, continually reduced by the winegrowers, were visible above ground.

These descriptions are of particular interest because it was in this place that Axel Munthe, according to what he writes in The Story of San Michele, during his first visit to Capri in 1876 saw old Mastro Vincenzo dig up *roba di Timberio* from the vineyard which many years later was to become the garden of the Villa San Michele. In this garden are now to be seen the few remains of the Roman villa which have escaped destruction, namely: a corner of what was probably a portico, with a painted back wall, and remains of a *cubiculum,* a little bedroom with wall paintings and mosaic floor.

Other ruins of Roman villas, now even more destroyed or completely annihilated, were registered by Feola and Mangoni in various parts of the wide area sloping down towards the north-western coast of the island: at Fravicina near the road leading to Migliara, at Pastino, Lercaro, Timberino, Rio delle Grotte, Monticello, Veterino, at Pozzo, which got its name from a vaulted Roman cistern, and at Damecuta on the north-west corner of the island, where farmers had always much ado smashing and clearing away marble floors, columns and capitals to make room for their crops. Finally, there is the so-called Villa Gradola or Gradelle, whose ruins lie above the Grotta Azzurra: here the American South-States Colonel John Clay MacKowen in 1875-76 dug up fragments of statues, columns and marble floors; here Dr. Axel Munthe found two small columns of variegated marble, one of which was unfortunately dropped into the sea, whereas the other one was safely brought to the Villa San Michele.

As is seen from the reports cited, there were on Capri many more villas than the twelve ascribed to Tiberius. This is not surprising, since in addition to the distinguished villas which served as residence for the Emperor, his guests and staff, there were obviously also those which primarily served for food supply, what the Romans called *villae rusticae* or *fructuariae*. The villa at Tiberino seems to have had a workshop which provided the more distinguished villas with expensive inlay decoration of onyx, agate and jasper, to judge from the mass of ornaments cut from these semi-precious stones which, according to Ignazio Cerio, were discovered among these ruins.

It is only in the 20th century, however, and thanks to the great energy and organizing ability of Amedeo Maiuri, sometime Director of the Museo Archeologico Nazionale in Naples, that the ruins of the three largest imperial villas on Capri have been excavated and studied in a satisfactory, scientific way: the Villa Jovis through excavations and surveying carried out in the years 1932-35, the Palazzo a Mare through surveying of the remains still accessible in 1935, and the Villa di Damecuta during excavations made between 1937 and 1948.

Of these three villas, Palazzo a Mare is considered to have been the one that Augustus preferred during his stays on Capri, for several reasons. It lay near Anacapri's eastern cliff, benefitting by its afternoon shade, protected from the hated *umidus auster,* the umid south wind which the Italians call scirocco, and near the ancient harbour, remains of which exist under water west of Marina Grande. The location of this villa was chosen with care, considering Augustus' delicate health which Suetonius tells a lot about (Aug. 81-82), saying among other things that he suffered from catarrh when exposed to a south wind and tolerated both cold and heat badly. He therefore always wore several articles of clothing under his toga in the winter and when out-of-doors always wore a broad-brimmed hat to protect him from the sun; and when travelling in a sedan always wanted to go slowly and take frequent rests.

Unfortunately, Palazzo a Mare is one of the most devastated Roman villas on Capri. After the ruins were deprived of their remaining marble floors and columns by Hadrawa, they were even more destroyed between 1806 and 1815 by the French and English troops who used their central part, which was surrounded by support walls, as a drill-ground and turned their eastern section into a fort with casemates and batteries. The fort in turn was converted into a private dwelling called Il Fortino, and later on other private houses were also built within the grounds of the villa. Nothing exists today of the constructions that Hadrawa discovered and plundered, such as the round building which he thought had been a temple, an exedra with a marble floor and a marble staircase leading up to it. Some foundation walls with rows of archways in a lemon grove and along a terrace to the west of it — that's about all what is left today of this vast palace.

Maiuri's investigations, however, made it clear that the villa, in addition to the eastern part, which probably was the Emperor's dwellings, and the central section, which was more likely a raised garden than a palestra, also included four cisterns for the water supply, and with its terraces, parks and promenades encompassed roughly an area a half-mile (800 meters) long, from the ancient harbour all the way to the ruins called Bagni di Tiberio. These are the best preserved part of the villa and are thought to be the remains of an extension made in Tiberius' time, intended for bathing and fish breeding. The ruins are on and below the steep coast bank which is kept in place by a mighty retaining wall with a large apse. Out in the water are remains of massive walls which perhaps formed a big basin or a small harbour.

The best preserved and most impressive of all the imperial villas on Capri raises its ruins above dreadful precipices on the highest point of the north-east corner of the island, 1095 feet (334 meters) above the narrow sound that separates it from the cape of the Sorrento peninsula (Fig. 5). The isolated and dominant position of this palace, allowing the eye to scan the Bay, the harbour and the whole eastern part of the island, its narrow corridors and rows of rooms disposed in a square around four water cisterns large as if to defy a siege, its small entry hall placed in the south-western corner of the complex — all this gives the building the character of a fortress, which along with the existence of the ancient lighthouse nearby very early led to its identification, undoubtably correct, as the Villa Jovis (Figs. 6-8). It must have been from this high cliff that Tiberius gazed towards the mainland for the signals which would inform him of how the action against Sejanus was progressing, and it must have been in this palace that he shut himself up for nine months after the traitor's fall, for reasons of security. And it is no doubt this palace Pliny had in mind when describing Capri in his Naturalis Historia (3, 82) as the island made famous by Tiberius' fortress: *Tiberi principis arce nobiles Capreae.* In all probability, Tiberius himself chose the location for this palace and instructed his architect about its plan and erection.

When Maiuri carried out his excavation of the ruin, there was hardly more left after the ancient plunderings than the naked walls of *opus caementicium,* the Roman concrete, made of a mixture of rough stones and lime mortar, with divisional horizontal courses of brickwork and, in places, a facing in *opus reticulatum,* consisting of small pyramidal blocks set point-inwards in such a way that the diagonal joints form a network. To get an idea of how these rooms and walls were once decorated, you have to look at the above-mentioned marble floor in the church of Santo Stefano (Fig. 9), at the pieces of sculpture that Feola had the good luck to find (Figs. 15, 18), and at the fragments of wall paintings which are reproduced in Alvino's and Quaranta's incomplete work on Le antiche ruine di Capri, published in 1835. The massiveness and remoteness of the palace, on the other hand, plus the existence of the chapel of Santa Maria del Soccorso within its area, are probably the main reasons for the fact that the walls themselves have escaped such destruction as the other imperial villas on Capri have suffered. This has enabled us to get a clear picture of the layout and erection of the palace almost in its entirety, and to relegate the romantic reconstructions made by the German architect C. Weichardt and others to the cabinet of archaeological curiosities.

The steep and irregular formation of the rock and, probably, Tiberius' strict orders, evidently forced his achitect, unknown to us, to concentrate the principal parts of the complex in one main building of three of four storeys, raised on terraces around four huge water cisterns partially hewn out of the bedrock, each of which was divided into two or three sections for the purification of the rain water which was gathered from the vaults of the cisterns and from the roofs of the surrounding parts of the palace (Fig. 8).

The use of these parts has been recognized, with varying degrees of certainty. On the south side, in addition to the entrance hall in the south-west corner, there is a typical Roman bath, with the four subdivisions called *apodyterium* (changing room), *frigidarium* (cold bath room), *tepidarium* (warm air room) and *calidarium* (hot air room). These are recognizable from traces of marble-clad bath tubs and remains of floor supports, so-called *suspensurae*, as well as from large tiles used for wall facing, which were called *tegulae mammatae*, being equipped with small projections, or « breasts ». These tiles and the floor supports allowed warm air from the central furnaces to circulate under the floors and in the walls. The furnaces also warmed the water which was led to the bath tubs from the nearest cistern.

The west side, which now is the most destroyed part of the palace, originally was the tallest, with storage rooms, partly subterranean, and above these two or possibly three storeys, each with a row of identical rooms along a narrow corridor. This plus the remains of an outside kitchen and pantries indicate that this part was inhabited by the servants.

The east side contained a wider corridor which gave access, through an equally wide room between two narorw and two square rooms, to an apse curving out towards the precipice on the highest natural point of the palace. This area served perhaps as the Emperor's offices and audience room. It was here that Feola, in 1827, found the sculptures mentioned above.

The northern section of the palace, the most isolated and most labyrinthine one, was undoubtedly the Emperor's private, well-guarded residence. From here he could ascend to the outlook where now the chapel of Santa Maria del Soccorso stands. From the same section a ramp leads up to an *ambulatio*, a long loggia for promenades, offering a magnificent view over the Bay, and provided with rooms for rest at either end and a *triclinium*, an open summer dining room, in the middle.

Just to the west of this loggia is a ruined building with narrow corridors between walls up to 13 feet (4 meter) thick. It is uncertain what this building was used for. Maiuri considered it to be the substruction for a *specularium*, from which observations of the stars were made for the astrological calculations with which Tiberius was so obsessed.

With its excavated main building and the surrounding buildings belonging to it, the Villa Jovis covers the entire top area of Monte Tiberio, more than 8,400 square yards (7000 sq.m.); but with its parks and gardens it certainly extended far down the slope towards the south-west. Part of the villa was also the lighthouse, Pharus, south of the main building. Its most important function was to transmit fire signals at night and smoke signals during the day to a similar lighthouse on the point of the Sorrento peninsula and to another one whose ruins have been discovered above the harbour of Misenum, where the Roman navy was based. These lighthouses must have played an important role in the signal system which quickly relayed news from Rome to Capri, especially during the critical days prior to Sejanus' fall.

Keeping this role in mind, one can understand why it was considered an omen when, according to Suetonius (Tib. 74), the Pharus on Capri collapsed during an earthquake just a few days before Tiberius' death. It must have been restored, however, for during the reign of Domitian, 30-40 years later, Capri was described by the poet Statius (Silvae, 3, 5, 100-101) as the island with the lighthouse, « the home of the Teleboans, where for fearful seamen Pharus lifts its mild light like the wandering moon of the night »:

Teleboumque domos, trepidis ubi dulcia nautis
lumina noctivagae tollit Pharus aemula lunae.

The Pharus consists of a tower about 52 feet (16 m.) high, as preserved, with a square, brickfaced base of concrete. At its north-west corner are remains of a pillar and an arch which once carried a viaduct leading up to a ledge from where probably a flight of steps gave access to the platform from which the fire and smoke signals were sent. While the imperial palace itself was left to crumble during the Middle Ages, the lighthouse was kept in working condition up to the 17th century, its fires being sometimes maintained by hermits who lived in the ruins. During Hadrawa's excavations and even later, a three-foot high layer of ash and charcoal gave testimony to the long service of the Pharus for the benefit of sea travel.

The third of the imperial villas investigated by Maiuri on Capri is situated on the north-west corner of the island within a flat area called Damecuta, and marked by a medieval watch-tower. The ruins of this villa, reduced by farmers for centuries and still more devastated by fortification work during the Napoleonic wars, were searched for marbles by MacKowen and Dr. Munthe in the late 19th century (above, p. 73) but since neither of them registered their finds we cannot pick out, among the pieces of ancient sculpture preserved in the Casa Rossa and in the Villa San Michele, exactly what items may come from this place. Dr. Munthe, who acquired the tower and surrounding area, donated both to the Italian State, thus making it possible for Maiuri to excavate what remained of the ruins.

The remains are few but interesting. Along the edge of the cliff facing the sea runs an *ambulatio,* supported by arches and composed of an inner loggia with niches for benches and an outer, more narrow loggia which had a roof carried by columns and also encircled an apse in what was perhaps the main part of the villa. At the opposite end of this double loggia, on the steep slope below the tower, are remains of several small rooms, of which the two farthest down are thought to have been a bedroom and an ante-room, with a little terrace. In the ante-room the excavators found a beautiful marble torso of a youth, perhaps a Narcissus (Fig. 20), which had escaped the fate of being broken up to be used as building stone or thrown into a lime-kiln; it is now preserved in the Certosa monastery. Keeping in mind Tiberius' passion for lovely Greek works of art, attested by Pliny (above, p. 51), Maiuri rightly identified these isolated rooms as the Emperor's inner sanctum. The excavators also found a bank of volcanic ash, heaped up against the loggia walls. This indicates that the villa must have been seriously damaged during the eruption of Vesuvius in 79 A.D. and abandoned ever since.

Like the Villa Jovis, this villa was remotely situated, fitting Tiberius' temperament. It could of course be reached by the « Phoenician Steps » and by a road which probably went approximately like the old mule track from Anacapri. But it was quicker and more comfortable to go by boat from Bagni di Tiberio to Punta di Gradola (or delle Gradelle) just east of the Grotta Azzurra, where traces exist, or existed, of steps cut into the rock. They led up towards the Roman villa whose ruins now are called Villa Gradola or Gradelle, and from which the way to the Villa di Damecuta is short.

It is uncertain if the name Gradola, which was once the name of the now-famous grotto as vell, is derived from Latin *gradus,* step, and thus refers to the above-mentioned stairs, or if it is a distorted diminutive form of Italian *grotta,* developed from Latin *crupta,* which is the Greek *krypta,* meaning something hidden.

The many caves and grottoes opening in Capri's cliffs, mostly at water level, but also higher up, were of course thought to have been the sites of the sexual orgies ascribed to Tiberius by malicious slanderers. The simple truth, however, is probably that he, like many other Romans of his time and later, liked to rest in such cool, dark and mysterious caverns in the bowels of the earth.

Greeks and Romans alike worshipped the spirits of nature in caves, and especially the water nymphs. Pan himself, called Faunus by the Romans, had an old cult place in Rome, in a cave below the western corner of the Palatine. At this cave, named Lupercal, Romulus and Remus were said to have been suckled by the she-wolf. Dionysius of Halicarnassus, a Greek rhetor and historian who lived in Rome during the reign of Augustus, reports in his Roman History (1, 79, 8) that there was an old bronze statue of the wolf and the twins in the fenced-in area outside the cave, which was « built up against the side of the Palatine ». Since in the autobiographical account of his accomplishments, the Res Gestae Divi Augusti, Augustus names Lupercal among those buildings he had restored, it is probable that the cave during his reign received a monumental entrance and a corresponding interior decoration.

This transformation of Lupercal's natural form in something typically Roman. The Romans loved to while away the hours in caves, particularly by the sea, not to delight in a romantic simplicity, but rather to enjoy the coolness of these caverns from comfortable couches, imbibe of the fresh water which often welled up there, and gaze at the beautiful view of the sea in front of them. The most notable example of such a converted cave may be seen at the coast between Terracina and Gaeta, near a little town whose name, Sperlonga, recalls that of an imperial villa called *Spelunca,* « The Cave », where Sejanus, according to Suetonius (Tib. 39) and Tacitus (Ann. 4, 59)), shielded Tiberius from falling rocks with his own body. The ruins of the villa lie in front of a cave whose interior contains a round artificial pool and whose mouth opens onto a larger rectangular pool outside, in the middle of which is a platform where one could recline at dinner and enjoy both the fish bred in the pools and the large groups of sculptures which were erected inside the cave: the huge Polyphemus in wine-drowned sleep while Odysseus and his men prepare to drive the stake into his eye, the monstrous Skylla and Odysseus' shipwreck, Menelaus with Patroclus' corpse, Odysseus and Diomedes with the sacred image of Athena. The recovery and restoration of these groups, which are signed by the masters of the Laocoon group, the Rhodian sculptors Athanodorus, Agesandrus and Polydorus, are one of the greatest archaelogical achievements of modern times.

One must keep in mind Lupercal and the Sperlonga cave in order to correctly understand in what way and for what purpose many of the caves on Capri were furnished during Tiberius' long stay on the istand.

First, it is important to point out that the meticulous examination of all the caves of Capri in the 40's by the Austrian spelaeoligist G. Kyrle led to the confutation of many older theories about them, primarily the assertion by Oppenheim, Furchheim and others that the north coast of the island in Tiberius' time was about 19 1/2 feet (6 meters) higher above sea level than today, that during the succeeding centuries it sank about 36 feet (11 meters) and then rose 12 feet (5 meters). In historical times, Capri's rocks have not undergone the risings and fallings which the volcanic ground around Pozzuoli was and still is subjected to. The coast line of the island in antiquity was almost as it is now, and in the Blue Grotto one could be just as astonished in Tiberius' time at seeing one's hand shining blue-white in the water as tourists are today, since the sunlight then as now forced its way through the water by the large opening which lies under the narrow entrance at water level. Kyrle has also shown that this entrance is not man-made, as Mac Kowen claimed, but a natural opening which was probably enlarged a little by paring off the rock around it.

That the water in the Grotta Azzurra stood at approximately the same level in Roman times as now is seen as well by the fact that the westernmost of the three passages which from the back wall of the cave lead into a large rock gallery of unknown length, first explored, partially, by Antonino Mazzarella, had its opening converted into a moorage for boats by being planed off and filled in with Roman masonry.

According to a deep-rooted tradition, mentioned already by August Kopisch, the « discoverer » of the cave in 1826 (see below, p. 135), these passages go right up to the imperial villa at Damecuta or to the Villa Gradola, so that Tiberius could sneak down to his orgies in the cave unseen. This claim gives evidence only of an imagination divorced from reality and must be emphatically refuted, if for no other reason because the air in the rock gallery is vitiated and dangerous to inhale.

Tiberius no doubt entered the grotto by boat, easier, as will be seen, than the tourists of today, and we know precisely what he saw in its interior. In 1964 divers succeded in rising two Roman marble statues from the bottom of the cave. Both of them are broken, eroded by the salt water, and covered all over with hard lime deposits, but in spite of this, one of them can be identified as a sea-god and the other as a Triton (Fig. 21). And in 1975 other Roman marbles were brought to light from the water in the grotto: a statue of a bearded sea-god, perhaps Neptun (Fig. 22), the lower part of a merman, with legs in the shape of curved fish tails, the upper part of a similar statue, and a small, draped female figure. The statue of the bearded sea-god and that of the merman are finished off at knee-height in the form of a base projecting at the back, and these bases were once inserted into niches hewn out in the natural walls of the cave. Since the niches are about 4 feet (c. 1, 20 m.) below the present surface of the water, it may be inferred that in Tiberius' time the water level was almost as much lower, so that the deities of the sea seemed to rise from the depths to greet the visiting Emperor.

The discovery of these statues confirms and explains a tale which Kopisch heard and recorded, but which before 1964 was regarded as fantasy. According to this tale, two priests about 1600 had swum into the cave but made a hasty retreat, terrified by the strange colour of the water and by the sight of the interior of the cave, which seemed to them like a lofty temple with a high altar and idols round about. Undoubtedly what the priest saw were the statues now recovered, plus other similar ones which perhaps are still lying on the bottom of the cave under some 70 feet (21 m.) of water.

Many other caves on Capri were transformed in Roman times, usually by being provided with semicircular stone benches along the back, carved out niches in the walls, and mosaic floors. Remains of such interior decoration are, or were, to be seen in the Grotta dell'Arco and in the Grotta Castiglione, both of which open their mighty mouths high up in sheer cliffs

and, therefore, preserve traces as well of having been used as
refuges, fortified and difficult to reach, during the centuries of
Saracen invasions.

The Grotta di Matromania, situated in a secluded place
north of Monte Tuoro, was also made into a nymphaeum, with
apses, a pool, and an arched ceiling with ornaments in mosaic
and stucco, as shown by explorations carried out by Maiuri
and Mingazzini. According to Feola and Mangoni, Hadrawa
found slabs from a marble floor, heads and arms of marble
statues, and a terracotta statuette with a Phrygian cap in this
cave. Hadrawa himself reports that an altar was discovered
there, which he says came to the British Museum. The two last-
mentioned finds combined with the name Matromania, which
is old and no fruit of scholarly speculation, led Mingazzini to
the assumption that the cave during Tiberius' time served as a
nymphaeum, but after the Emperor's death was really used, as
many earlier scholars claimed, as a cult place for Cybele, the
Anatolian goddess also called Mater Magna, the Great Mother.
This theory, in any case, is more acceptable than the one claim-
ing that Mithras was worshipped in this cave, for the statement that the relief showing the god sacrificing the bull (above,
p. 65, Fig. 19) was found near the cave is far from reliable,
the cave itself lacks the mysterious darkness of Mithraic sanctuaries, and its other name, Mitromania, is a distortion due to
the belief that the cave did serve as a Mithraeum.

Remains of Roman masonry are also to be seen in the
Grotta dell'Arsenale at the beach south-east of Castiglione. This
cave was also decorated with mosaics, remnants of which were
discovered during an exploration in 1879. According to Mangoni, a nautical instrument of iron was found there, which can
mean that in later days the cave was really used ad an arsenal
or boatyard, as the name suggests.

Hadrawa and Secondo state that Roman masonry was also to be seen in and around the Grotta Oscura, a cave which
was considered by many later authors as being identical with
the Grotta Azzurra, despite the fact that it was clearly de-

scribed by Fabio Giordano and J. Addison as being situated on the south coast of the island not far from the Faraglioni. The mistake is perhaps explainable since the Grotta Oscura, according to a note by Feola, disappeared from sight in 1808 due to a land slide, which claimed a donkey and the tower of the Certosa monks, and completely hid the entrance to the cave.

The specimens of ancient sculpture which have come down to us from the ruins of the Roman villas and the waters of the Blue Grotto were certainly widely surpassed by a statue whose existence is known only through a square base of red marble, so-called rosso antico, with the inscription (IGI 898) ΑΘΑΝΟΔΟΡΟΣ ΑΓΗΣΑΝΔΡΟΥ ΡΟΔΙΟΣ ΕΠΟΙΗΣΕ. The base, which according to Mangoni was found in 1823 near San Valentino on the north slope of Castiglione, according to others, near Santa Maria del Soccorso, and which according to Norman Douglas was sent to New York, bore a statue now lost, signed by Athanodoros, son of Agesandros, from Rhodes. Thus, the sculptor belonged to the same family of artists whose workshop produced the famous Laocoon group, which according to Pliny's Naturalis Historia (36, 37) is a work by Agesander, Polydorus and Athanodorus from Rhodes, and also the magnificent groups discovered in Tiberius' cave at Sperlonga, which are signed by Athanodoros son of Hagesandros, Hagesandros son of Paionios, and Polydoros son of Polydoros. Since the same names were usually passed down from generation to generation in Greek artist families, we cannot with any certainty establish if the master of the lost statue on Capri was the same Athanodoros as the sculptor who worked on the Laocoon group and/or the Sperlonga groups. What one may dare to believe, however, is that Tiberius himself acquired the Capri statue on Rhodes, where he lived for seven whole years.

A discovery of particular interest was made in 1922 on the site of the imperial villa on the north slope of Castiglione, where a farmer's hoe unearthed a bronze statuette of an Egyptian Pharao (Fig. 10) which had escaped Hadrawa's treasure hunters. This statuette, and the fragments of Egyptian statues mentioned above (pp. 36, 70), are important proof that the interest in Egyptian religion and art which the Romans evinced, particularly after Egypt was incorporated into the Roman Empire, manifested itself even on Capri.

Capri had the honour of being adorned with imperial villas and being the permanent residence of Tiberius for eleven years — a dangerous honour, according to what many contemporaries may have thought. But the island was not given the honour of housing Tiberius' ashes, which were entombed in Augustus' mausoleum in Rome. Nor is it likely that many of the two Emperors' companions and employees were buried on Capri, with the exception of Masgaba, native officials like the *agoranómoi,* and servants like Julia Aphrodisia, one of Augustus' freedwomen, who on her epitaph (Eph. epigr., Add. ad CIL, X, 671) is also called Veneria, perhaps because she had been a servant in the temple of Venus Erycina in Rome.

The graves that have been found on the island as a rule contained the remains of uncremated dead and simple grave gifts. Among the oldest are two graves near Ceselle, Anacapri, from which Antonino Mazzarella, in 1915, saved clay vases of late Republican date and a so-called lachrymal vase of glass.

A large burial ground seems to have stretched from the church of San Costanzo up towards the site of the present-day cemetries of the town of Capri. This necropolis was clearly used for many centuries, to judge from the discovery in it of the « Etruscan » vases, bronze candelabras, clay lamps and painted Italo-Greek vases mentioned above, as well as simple graves from much later times. Mangoni reports that near Le Parate several hundred simple graves were discovered, each one close to the next, and each one consisting of some large roof tiles placed over the dead like a roof ridge. Each skeleton had a little clay vase at its feet, two nails on its head, and a bronze coin of imperial minting in its mouth. Unfortunately, Mangoni says nothing of the coin portraits, which could have given information about the date of the graves.

86

Their poorness indicates that they belonged to indigent people who probably lived during the late Empire, to judge from the fact that a similar grave now to be seen in the garden of the Villa San Michele must have been placed there after the imperial villa on Capodimonte was abandoned and had reached an advanced state of ruin.

A noteable contrast to these poor burials is a large limestone sarcophagus which was found « in scanty depth » in 1810 just west of San Costanzo and now stands on the terrace of the Albergo Grotta Azzurra not far from there. The discovery is described by Mangoni, but his somewhat antiquated Italian was misunderstood by Beloch and Mingazzini to the extent that they talk about a gable-roofed chamber tomb hewn out of the living rock — a type of tomb that never existed on Capri. The lid of the sarcophagus has the form of a gable-roof, with a fish scale design on the front slope; the front of the chest is decorated with a flat medallion flanked by two garlands and two winged Gorgon's heads, the corners with bull heads, the short sides each with a garland and a rosette, while the back is undecorated. The sarcophagus contained the skeleton of a woman, remains of her clothing woven with interspersed gold and silver threads, two bracelets and two earrings of gold, a cameo ring, a sceptre wound with three gold bands, and in the mouth of the skeleton, a gold coin with the portrait of Vespasian. These expensive grave gifts, of whose whereabouts Mangoni says nothing, indicate that the dead woman was a distinguished lady, which led to the facile assumption that she was Crispina, the unfortunate consort of Commodus (cf. above, p. 63). This is contradicted, however, by the roughly worked sarcophagus, which surely was made in a later time than hers, while the gold coin merely shows that the lady died at some time after its minting — gold coins were often treasured for a long time.

The island must have offered a unique sight for those who during the last years of Tiberius' reign and the next few centuries after sailed over the Bay of Naples towards Capri. The bold formation of the cliffs was the same as today, the green of the woods and fields was perhaps as luxuriant as now, but on top of these cliffs and out of this greenness rose the imperial palaces, more impressive than the largest hotels of today. Over the precipice in the east brooded « Tiberius' fortress », darkened by terrible rumours. From the palace of Augustus near the harbour, the gaze could ascend from one magnificent villa to the next up towards the Greek wall of the little town and the hill peaks in the background. On the top of the mountain above the dizzying, zigzaging steps made by Greeks in an already distant past, one could glimpse the imperial villa which almost two thousand years later would be succeded by Axel Munthe's Villa San Michele. And far out on the island's western corner one saw the other remote palace to which Tiberius loved to retreat. There is not much of poetic exaggeration in the two lines which, probably incorrectly, have been ascribed to the poet Statius, a native of Naples, picturing Capri as « a small island, but once a rival of Rome, worthy of receiving even Caesarean men »:

Insula parva quidem, quondam tamen aemula Romae
Caesaribusque viris hospita digna fuit.

MEDIEVAL CAPRI

In the majority of cases we do not know how long the imperial villas of Capri were kept in repair and inhabited. The only certain fact is that the one at Damecuta was abandoned already after the eruption of Vesuvius in 79 A.D. Others perhaps were left to decay during the later centuries of the Empire. The earthquake of 366 certainly started the long process of disintegration for all of them.

At that time the decline of the Roman Empire had also begun. A capable but totally uneducated officer from Pannonia named Valentinian resided in Milan as Emperor of the western part of the Empire, but was primarily occupied with wars against the Saxons, Alamanni, Franks and other invading Germanic tribes. His equally uneducated brother Valens reigned from Constantinople over the eastern half of the Empire, fighting to repel invasions of Persians and Goths. Fifty years before, Christianity had become an officially recognized religion, whose followers were deep in conflict among themselves over the question of whether Christ was of the same or of a similar essence as the Father.

Valentinian died at Carnuntum in 375 of apoplexy incurred during a fit of anger while he was preparing a death-blow to the Quadi on the other side of the Danube. Valens lost his life three years later in a crushing defeat against the Goths near Adrianople. Soon almost the entire Germanic world was on the move, with the invading Huns at the rear.

We do not know how informed the inhabitants of Capri could have been about these battles, nor what repercussions they may have felt from the dramatic events happening nearer home: when the Visigoths invaded Italy under Alaric and plundered Rome in 410, when the Vandals conquered Carthage, Sardinia and Corsica and under Gaiseric subjected Rome to an even worse plundering in 455, and when in 476 the Western Roman Empire ceased to exist after the Germanic chief Odoacer deposed the young Emperor Romulus Augustulus, who died shortly afterwards at his home of exile, the villa of Lucullus, situated on Pizzofalcone and the little island which now supports the medieval Castel dell'Ovo in Naples.

But they could hardly have missed hearing how in 537 Naples despite its mighty Roman walls was captured from the Ostrogoths by the Byzantine Emperor Justinian's famed general, Belisarius, who had his soldiers crawl into the city at night through a cut and dried-up aqueduct, as described by the contemporary historian Procopius, in his history of the Gothic War in Italy (5, 8-9). The Goths, it is true, retook Naples six years later, but after their state had dissolved, the city came under Byzantine rule for over two hundred years.

In his chronicle of the Montecassino monastery, written in the 12th century and preserved in the monastery's library (Codex 518), the Benedictine monk Petrus Diaconus says that a Roman patrician named Tertullus donated *insulam Caprariam in salo neapolitano locatam* to St Benedict (480-547) and that the gift was confirmed by Emperor Justinian. Capraria is the ancient name for the little island between Corsica and the coast of Tuscany which is now called Capraia, but the addition « situated in Neapolitan waters » shows that Capri is meant; the names of the two islands were often confused. The authenticity of the donation, however, has been doubted, since Gregory the Great, Pope from 590 to 696, in a letter to Bishop John of Sorrento orders him to go to the monastery of Santo Stefano on Capri with the bones of the martyred Agatha, which indicates that at that time the island was under the ecclesiastical jurisdiction of the Bishop of Sorrento and not of the monks of Montecassino.

The monastery of Santo Stefano was most likely situated near the present-day piazza of the town of Capri, where the

90

church still bears the martyr's name; it is possible that the campanile in this piazza formed part of the monastery.

In secular matters, Capri was for some time subject to the Duchy of Naples, which from the end of the 6th century was a bulwark against the Longobards in Campania and in 763 changed allegiance from the Byzantine Emperor to the Pope and its official language from Greek to Latin. In the 9th century, perhaps through an act of the Emperor of the Holy Roman Empire, Louis II, the island became subject to Amalfi, a fact which is confirmed both by contemporary documents and through the existence of Amalfitan family names on Capri.

During these centuries, however, the Longobards, the Byzantines and the independent city-states in southern Italy were confronted with a terrible enemy. Since the dawn of history, the Mediterranean had been the haunt of pirates. Etruscan pirates had terrorized the Greek colonists, and during the two last centuries of the Roman Republic, well-organized pirate fleets, based on the south coast of Asia Minor and later on the north coast of Africa, caused serious damage to sea trade and travel by seizing ships and cargoes, demanding ransoms for prisoners or else selling them as slaves, defeating Roman fleets and raiding the very shores of Italy, from Brundisium all the way up to Ostia — until Pompey the Great, with all Roman military resources at his disposal, was able to eliminate this menace from the waters and coasts both of the Mediterranean and the Black Sea.

Now the old plague returned, and stayed much longer than before. The Moslem Saracens during the 9th century captured Sicily; and from bases on this island and the northern coast of Africa they began to ravage the Apennine peninsula. The Longobard Dukes in Benevento, Capua and Salerno, busy squabbling among themselves, were unable to repel these Arabian pirates, who installed themselves on the promontory of Agropolis south of Paestum and by the mouth of the Liri, north of Gaeta, plundered the Montecassino monastery and the basilicas of St Peter and St Paul in Rome, carried off tens of thousands of city inhabitants to slavery and caused people dwelling along the coastal areas to abandon their homes and fields for fear of falling victim to the same fate. In Sicily, it is true, the Saracen rulers can be remembered as the patrons of olive cultivation and agriculture, silk production, merchandise and literature, but on the mainland they are remembered only with dread and horror. « *Saraceno* is still a common term of abuse », says Norman Douglas in his Old Calabria.

The navies of Naples, Sorrento and Amalfi fought bloody battles against the pirates and occasionally won glorious victories. In 920 the Neapolitans succeeded in annihilating a Saracen fleet in a sea battle in the Bay and captured the majority of its crew. Only one of the pirate ships escaped and unwisely took refuge in Capri, where the islanders had the satisfaction of slaying these enemies down to the last man.

The Capriotes seem to have been protected from the Saracens, to a certain degree, by their poverty, which made their island less tempting to the pirates. But above all they relied on St Constantius. According to Philippus Ferrarius' catalogue of Saints, he was of imperial lineage and Bishop of Constantinople. How and why he came to Capri is shrouded in the mists of time. According to one legend, his earthly remains came drifting across the ocean to the island in a wine cask. But the above-mentioned Sermo de transitu Sancti Constantii (p. 26) says that he died on Capri and was buried in the church above the harbour which bears his name, San Costanzo. This much is certain that he became Capri's patron saint, at first equal with and then more popular than its former patron saint, St Severin.

Constantius' church was rebuilt in late Byzantine style, probably in the 12th century, when it was given a ground plan in the form of a Greek cross, with vaults and high arches supported by four columns taken from a Roman villa and placed one at each of the inner corners (Fig. 24). This church is architecturally akin to many others in the old Byzantine

92

world, especially the famous Cattolica near Stilo in Calabria. Together with the early Christian chapel built into a Roman cistern on Monte San Michele (p. 69) and the little church of Sant'Anna in the town of Capri (Fig. 25), it is the oldest Christian sanctuary on the island.

How San Costanzo protected his island is recorded in the Sermo de transitu Sancti Constantii and in the Sermo de virtute Sancti Constantii, two sermons transcribed in 1174 by the Benedictine monk Marinus in the monastery of San Severino in Naples and now kept in the Biblioteca Nazionale of that city (XIV-H-37).

In the year of our Lord 991, we are told in these pious homilies, a Saracen fleet under the command of the iniquitous and perfidious Boalim ravaged the region around Amalfi and then sailed into the Bay of Naples. After the infidels had tried in vain to come ashore at Stabiae and Naples and their attack on Ischia had failed, they decided towards evening to sail across the Bay towards Capri. But all of a sudden, a frightful storm broke out, the star-speckled sky became covered with clouds, hail as big as stones lashed the ships, and a violent wind blew them far south towards the coast of Lucania. At the same time, the inhabitants of Capri had fled to their hiding places in fear, all except an old woman who was not strong enough to flee. When she heard steps outside her house, she thought that the Saracens had come to kill her, but instead through the grace of God she saw two girded angel-like elderly men who said: « May it please you to know that we are Constantius and Severinus, the protectors of this island, and we have now defeated your enemies on the sea and driven the Saracen host away from here ».

In the beginning of the 11th century, however, the Longobards, the Byzantines and the Saracens all alike were confronted with the Viking descendants from Normandy, who topped them all in aggressiveness, ruthlessness and handiness with weapons. Under the leadership of five brothers and half-brothers of a family named Hauteville (Altavilla), of whom

Robert Guiscard and Roger are the most renowned, these Normans in less than a hundred years subdued the whole of southern Italy and Sicily, thereby putting an end to the Longobard duchies in Campania, the Byzantine domination in Apulia, and the Saracen rule in Sicily. All this while other Normans invaded and conquered England.

The Norman conquest, however, did not stop the Saracen piracy, and for the people of Capri this was a strain worse than when their island was captured by the Longobard prince Guaimario IV of Salerno, worse even than when the Norman king Roger II in 1133 retook the island after a rebellion against his rule. No fisherman on Capri could be sure that he would return home with his catch and not be caught by a Saracen ship and sold as a slave in Africa.

On the other hand, the claim that the settlement down by the harbour was abandoned and the population moved up within the old town's Greek walls because of the Saracen threat can hardly be considered credible. This is contradicted namely both by the site of the church of San Costanzo and by the Arabian geographer Edrisi, who on Roger II's commission drew a map of the world, engraved on a large silver plaque weighing 330 lbs. (150 kg.), with a commentary saying that « on Qabrah (Capri) there is a medium-large town, in whose midst a spring wells forth », which no doubt means the settlement by the harbour and the Fontana Truglio. The people who lived in this town may have trusted that when Saracen ships were sighted, they could get themselves and the church treasures into safety behind the upper town's wall and in the cave on Castiglione in time, and that San Costanzo would protect the island.

Through the marriage of Roger II's daughter Constance to Henry of Hohenstaufen, son of the Holy Roman Emperor Frederick I Barbarossa, and himself eventually to be Emperor Henry VI, the Norman empire in Italy came under the rule of the Hohenstaufen Emperors and was governed for over fifty years (1197-1250) by the greatest of them, Frederick II. A ruler who, through his knowledge and literary abilities, his concern for law, erudition and art, and his magnificent court at Lucera in Apulia, complete with harem and Saracen body-guard, came to be known as *Stupor Mundi,* « the Wonder of the World ». The code of laws he had drawn up and the concern he showed for the famous medical school in Salerno and the university he founded in Naples in 1224 belong to his greatest achievements. He was also before his time through his interest in preserving and collecting ancient sculpture. His son Manfred was an enlightened regent like his father, and i.a. had Aristotle translated to Latin, both from Arabian versions and directly from the Greek.

According to a document preserved in the Biblioteca Cuomo in Naples (XXVI-A-19), Frederick II in 1204 enfeoffed his justiciary Sergio Scrofa in Amalfi with « the island of Capri with the monastery of St Stephan and everything that belongs to it », for a yearly duty of nine gold solidi and a hundred barrels of wine. This fief seems to have been hereditary and was ratified by Charles I of Anjou, the brother of Louis IX of France, who in 1266 defeated Manfred and became king of Naples and Sicily.

The dissatisfaction with the French administration in Sicily, however, led to the terrible bloodbath known as the Sicilian Vespers, since at the chiming of the evening song bells in Palermo Easter Monday 1282, at least 8.000 Frenchmen are said to have been murdered. The Sicilians then offered their island to Peter III of Aragon, who was married to Manfred's daughter Constance. During the war which followed between Naples and Sicily, Capri was captured after two unsuccessful attempts by Peter's dreaded Catalan mercenaries. Not until Charles I had died and his son, also named Charles, who was held prisoner in Spain by Alfonso III of Aragon, had been freed and had taken the throne of Naples as Charles II, was there a truce in 1289 between him and Alfonso's younger brother James, who succeeded his father Peter as king of Sicily. But Capri, like Ischia and Procida, remained in Aragon hands

as an important naval base until 1299, when all three islands
were recaptured by Charles II. The Capriote Sergio de Nicola,
who successfully defended his island against the Aragonese
attacks in 1283 and 1284, and who after the capitulation in
1286 had to buy himself free with 16 ounces of gold, became
the commander of Capri's castle and successfully attended to
the fortification of the island. Not until 1302 was there peace
between the two kingdoms of Naples and Sicily.

A multitude of documents from the years 1266 to 1442,
when Naples was under the rule of the House of Anjou, give
us interesting glimpses into the conditions of Capri during
those centuries. A great many writs from the royal chancellery,
always in Latin, concern permissions of importation of food
to the island and remission of import duties, indicating that
Capri with its barren soil and insufficient supply of water was
not self-supporting, even though according to more than one
document, the town of Capri in the 1270's had only 124
fuochi, hearths or households.

During the reign of Charles II's successor, Robert the Wise
(1309-1343), the commander on Capri, as well as his colleagues
on Ischia and Procida and in Castellammare di Stabia, received
royal reminders about the necessity of always keeping watch
across the sea for enemy ships, and of lighting fire signals in
case such should be seen. The same king in 1313 ordered his
capitano in Amalfi to insist upon guarantees from certain specified Capriotes belonging to, among others, the famous families
Arcucci, Strina and Mazzarella that they would no longer molest
the Bishop of Capri, who because of their conspiracy had been
forced to leave the island. Twelve years later there was obviously an argument about where the Bishop should live, since
the King on November 8, 1325, wrote to the commander and
ordered him and the inhabitants of the town of Capri to allow
the Bishop to live freely and without hindrance *in ipsa civitate,*
in the town itself, as well in other places owned by the church
within the municipality, *dummodo loca ipsa suspecta non sint,
nec possint ex incursionibus hostium fidelibus nostris tam*

dampni vel incommodi verisimiliter immittere, that is: « if only these places are not unsafe and could not reasonably cause our faithful subjects injury or suffering due to enemy attacks ».

It is also of interest to note that the King in 1333, probably concerned about the earnings of his subjects, issued a decree forbidding coral fishing without royal permission *inter Caprum et minervam, ubi corallorum maxima copia invenitur,* that is, between Capri and the promontory of the Sorrento peninsula, still designated by its pagan name, « where the greatest amount of corals are found », and where people from as far away as Marseilles came to fish them.

The next year, the inhabitants of Anacapri requested King Robert to free them from being subject to the town of Capri, but the reasons against it given by the town weighed heavier with the King, and he decreed *ut nihil innoveretur,* that nothing should be changed. This is the first time we hear of the antagonism between the two communities which was to last for centuries. In 1338 the King dispatched several decrees from which can be understood that the Anacapriotes protested partly because the participants in their traditional procession to the church of San Costanzo on Palm Sunday had been attacked by priests and laymen from the town of Capri, who smashed their cross and the pictures of San Costanzo and the Virgin Mary and flogged their women and priests until the blood flowed, and partly because the people from the town molested their women and old people while their young men were away working as shipbuilders and caulkers in the arsenal of Naples. They received scant help from the King, however, who merely enjoined them to fortify the entrance from the ancient steps and keep it guarded — provided that the expenses for this did not encroach on the taxes and fees he required.

Queen Joan I, who succeded King Robert to the throne of Naples in 1343, was more generous to the islanders. In November of that year, the regions around the Bay were devastated by a terrible storm whose horrors are described by

Petrarca, who saw them, in a letter to Cardinal Giovanni Colonna. Because of this disaster, the Queen allowed the Capriotes tax remission and free import of grain from Naples.

Of special importance for Capri was the goodwill she bore towards her secretary and minister Giacomo Arcucci, who belonged to an old, distinguished Capriote family. It is believed that this Arcucci or his family with the Queen's aid had the church of San Costanzo enlarged by adding a square presbytery on its south side, in doing which one also had the original entrance on the east side walled up and a new one made on the north side, where today, however, only the framework of the portal, enclosed in a modern façade, gives an example of the art of stonecarving of that time. The beautiful Byzantine interior, on the other hand, remains mostly unchanged, except for the granite columns which replace the ancient ones, removed in the 18th century (above, p. 71, and Fig. 24).

Giacomo Arcucci also founded a Franciscan monastery near Marina Grande, not far from a little church dedicated to San Severino, and had a citadel built by the piazza of Capri which was called Palazzo della Regina and today, rebuilt, is named Palazzo Cerio (Fig. 26). The Queen probably more than once resided in its rooms, which now contain the museum, library and consert hall of the Centro Caprense.

La Certosa, the Carthusian monastery founded by the same Arcucci in thanks for the birth of a long-desired son, was to have immeasurable importance for the island for over four hundred years. The monastery, dedicated to San Giacomo, the Apostle Jacob, was built in the valley between Castiglione and Monte Tuoro on ground donated by the Queen, perhaps over ruins of a Roman building. It was completed in 1374. Since then, it has undergone many changes, has been destroyed and rebuilt, enlarged and adorned; but it has also, after the expulsion of the monks in 1808, experienced a period of decline and decay, the damages of which are not yet healed by current restorations. With its small, 15th century cloister, whose arcades are supported by columns crowned in part with

98

Roman capitals, its single-nave church lightened from high Gothic windows, its large cloister added towards the end of the 16th century, in the form of a vast courtyard surrounded by porticos in late Renaissance style intended to carry a second storey never built, with its 17th century bell tower topped by a crown of baroque volutes, its refectory, kitchen and store-rooms, its suite of rooms reserved for the Prior, and its garden extending towards the precipice in the south, this monastery constitutes an important monument of art, embodying as well much of Capriote history for more than four centuries (Fig. 27). A fresco painted towards the end of the 14th century in the lunette over the portal leading from the atrium into the monastery church portrays the Virgin Mary with the Infant Jesus, surrounded by San Bruno and San Giacomo, Queen Joan with two ladies-in-waiting, and Giacomo Arcucci with two sons. Because of the great number of privileges granted them by the Queen and various Popes, the produce and labour that the islanders were obliged to give them, and the opportunities of work that this created, the monks obtained a dominant position on the island, more important than that of the Bishop and the poor priesthood of the churches.

This is also illustrated by a comparison between the large monastery and four small churches or chapels from the end of the 14th and the beginning of the 15th century. Thanks to the fact that later on bigger and more costly churches were built in Capri and Anacapri, these four were allowed to retain their original rusticity and genuine simplicity, without being « embellished » by later reconstructions. These churches are: Sant'Anna (Fig. 25), formerly Santa Maria delle Grazie, situated by the street of the same name in Capri, and distinguished by having in its interior two Roman stumps of columns with Corinthian capitals supporting a high Byzantine arch; Santa Croce by the Via Tiberio in Capri, a chapel called San Michele since 1802, when the early Christian chapel on the height with the same name was closed and abandoned (above, p. 69); Santa Maria di Costantinopoli, which was originally the main church of Anacapri; and Santa Maria di Cetrella, on the edge of Anacapri's precipice above Marina Piccola.

Queen Joan was famous for her beauty and notorious for her erotic adventures, for which she was chastised by Bridget of Sweden, when this lady and her two sons stayed with her for the second time while on a pilgrimage to the Holy Land in 1372. During this visit, Bridget's son Karl died. According to what Margareta Clausdotter says in her Chronicon de genere et nepotibus S. Brigittae, this son, to his mother's horror, started a love affair with the Queen at the presentation by kissing her on the mouth instead of on the foot as court etiquette prescribed. When Bridget on her return voyage to Rome once again stayed with Joan, who always welcomed her with kindness and respect, the plague was raging in Naples, and the Swedish seeress again castigated her hostess and those around her for the dissolution of morality at the court and in the city.

Bridget's words to the Queen, that her crown was made of straw, soon proved to be true. Joan was removed from the throne in 1381 by Charles of Durazzo and was murdered the next year. Her protégé Arcucci was deprived of all his property and lived his last years as a poor guest in the monastery he founded. He died in 1386 and was remembered by two epitaphs in the monastery church of which the longer and later one is on a marble monument representing the founder reclining and holding a model of the original building. This monument was moved in 1891 to the church of Santo Stefano. Its inscription has proved to contain some incorrect information, which is why Bishop Pellegrino (below, p. 110) is thought to have had reason to complain to the Holy See that the Certosa monks had set up an inscription altered for their own purposes and had desecrated the tomb of the monastery founder.

After the dethronement and death of Joan I, her successor Charles III and his son and heir Vladislav, who belonged to the Durazzo branch of the house of Anjou, had to fight for the crown against Louis I and Louis II of Anjou, who belonged to the Valois-Provence branch of the same house and therefore laid claim on the kingdom of Naples. A diary kept from 1380 to 1388 by Jean Le Fèvre, Bishop of Chartres and chancellor for the two pretenders, presents us with interesting information about the large amounts of money which were transferred from Provence to their followers on Capri, among others to the mayors of Capri and Anacapri, Oliviero Strina and Gazaro Cortese, who used the money to repair the walls of the town of Capri and to purchase gunpowder for mortars. After Charles III's victory over Louis I, three of the latter's followers on Capri were executed. But there must have been Capriotes loyal to the Durazzo branch as well, for during Vladislav's reign, the islanders thwarted a plot against the castle and, therefore, were praised for their *inconcussa fidelitas,* their unshakable loyalty, in a royal diploma dated March 12, 1408, and granted exemption from taxes and duties.

In 1414, Queen Joan II succeded her brother Vladislav to the throne of Naples. Fearing Louis III, the Anjou-Valois-Provence pretender to the same throne, she sought help from and adopted King Alfonso V of Aragon, Corsica and Sardinia, but then regretted it and took Louis' brother René as her heir, thereby setting the stage for a war between Alfonso and René. In this war too, Capri's importance as a base for attacks against Naples was obvious. While René was besieged in Naples by Alfonso, the island was delivered into the hands of the latter through a coup which is described, albeit with certain variations, by more than one author. The most complete and dramatic description is contained in the anonymous diary now called after a later owner Diurnali del Duca di Monteleone. According to this diary, on the 22nd of October, 1441, a priest from Capri came to Alfonso's camp in Capua and offered to deliver the island into the King's hands if he were given a back-up of two hundred foot-soldiers. He got them, and landed one night with them on Capri, obviously somewhere on the west coast. Led by the priest, the soldiers then captured Anna Crapa, i.e. Anacapri, crept down to Capri, probably along the path called Il Passatiello (p. 32), and occupied the town and its stronghold on Castiglione. Then they had the good fortune to be able to seize some ships on stop-over at Capri, loaded with badly needed grain for the besieged and starving Naples, or according to other sources, a galleon coming from France with 80,000 scudi for René. In any case, the result was that on July 1, 1442, the Aragonians captured Naples in the same way as Belisarius' troops did 905 years earlier: by entering the town through an old aqueduct. René was expelled, and Alfonso took the throne of the Kingdom of Naples.

Capri had played an important role in a decision of great historical consequence. Already the year before, Alfonso had relieved the taxes imposed on the islanders, confirmed the privileges granted to them by earlier rulers, and decreed that the island could not be enfeoffed, and that it should be ruled by a capitano appointed only for a year at a time.

The acts of violence perpetrated by foreign conquerors and Saracen pirates during the centuries of the Middle Ages seem to have made the inhabitants of Capri, as well as those of Ischia, hard and ruthless, judging from Fazio Uberti's geographical poem Dittamondo, composed between 1350 and 1360, in which he says of the islanders: « They who there live are quick to attack, and they who come there praise God if they escape without injury »:

> *Gli habitator vi son sùbiti e vàpoli.*
> *Lodano Iddio color che vi vanno,*
> *Se senza danno da lor son scapoli.*

CAPRI UNDER SPANISH RULE

Alfonso V of Aragon, who as ruler of the kingdom of Naples became Alfonso I, initiated the long political, economic and cultural dominance of the Spaniards in this kingdom: a dominance far too often characterized by oppression, extortion, misrule, bigotry, obscurantism and intrigues. The Spanish era lasted well into the 18th century, with a series of kings of the united Spain: Ferdinand the Catholic, the Emperor Charles V of Habsburg, in whose realm « the sun never set », three Habsburg kings named Philip, and finally Philip V of Bourbon.

Copies of decrees from the Aragonese kings, written in Latin, as well as, after 1504, resolutions issued from the chancellery and the Camera della Sommaria of the Spanish viceroys in Naples, written in clumsy bureaucratic Italian, interspersed with Latin, Spanish and vernacular words, give us sundry glimpses of the economic and administrative conditions of Capri during this era, of the islanders' struggle to make a living, and of their battle against injustices of various kinds. There are documents concerning wine export and silk production, taxes and duties, conflicts between the communities of Capri and Anacapri over fishing waters and between the Certosa monks and the coral fishermen over the monastery's claim of a tenth of their catch. The enmity between the two communities lessened somewhat, however, after Frederick II of Aragon had given equal status to both.

In addition to these documents concerning problems which to us may seem trivial but were quite important to the parties involved, there are others which show what reverberations the islanders felt of the more dramatic events in the world.

During the war between Charles V and Francis I, King of France, the Emperor in 1528 gave the viceroy of Naples permission to sell the island — despite the privileges granted by earlier rulers — for three thousand ducats to a Neapolitan named Paolo Pellegrino, who had repaired the walls of the town of Capri, erected a stronghold for the protection of Anacapri, and rendered great service when Naples was besieged by the French King's general, Odet de Foix, Vicomte de Lautrec.

When during this war Genoa enlisted on the French side and a Genoese fleet under the command of Filippino Doria sailed into the Bay of Salerno, a fleet manned with Spanish elite troops set sail from Naples to join battle with the Genoese. When the Spaniards sailed through the sound between the Sorrento Peninsula and Capri, their courage was fired by a Spanish monk and hermit named Consalvo Barretta, who left his cave and appeared on the cape called Punta del Monaco, prophesying a brilliant victory for his countrymen. He was a bad prophet, however, for the sea battle off Capo d'Orso east of Amalfi the 2nd of June, 1528, ended in a terrible defeat for the Spanish, who were for the most part slaughtered or drowned. The two Spanish commanders were sent to Genoa as prisoners but had the good fortune to escape being handed over to Francis, since the unscrupulous sea hero Andrea Doria, Genoa's strong man, suddenly found it advantageous to go over to Charles V.

The great Empire of Charles V, however, was threatened by yet another enemy, namely, the pirate fleets of the North African Barbary states, who carried on the Saracens' activities under the command of the Turkish Sultan Suliman II's dreaded admiral, Kheir-ed-Din, known as Barbarossa, « Redbeard ». He took Algiers from the Spaniards, and from there, in the years 1519 to 1535, made repeated attacks on Sicily and the west coast of the Apennine Peninsula, where he pillaged and burned and carried off thousands of people into slavery. The many watch towers, Torri di Guardia, which still stand along the coasts of the Mar Tirreno give witness to the terror that the Saracen and Turkish ships struck in the hearts of the inhabitants of these regions.

The importance of Capri as a base for attacks against Naples and the Sorrento Peninsula is proven once again by the fact that the pirates assailed the island no less than seven times during these years. The worst of these attacks was in 1535, when Kheir-ed-Din captured the town of Capri and burned the castle of Anacapri, the ruins of which ever since are known as Castello Barbarossa (Fig. 23). Because of these attacks, Charles V gave the inhabitants of Anacapri, and soon also those of the town of Capri, permission to bear arms.

In the same year of 1535, the Emperor sent a fleet of 500 ships with 30,000 soldiers to Tunis, where they conquered Kheir-ed-Din's forces and freed 20,000 Christian slaves. The Turkish sea power, however, was not destroyed. Kheir-ed-Din moved the scene of war to the west, devastated Mallorca and Menorca, plundered — in alliance with the French! — the city of Nice which at that time belonged to Savoy, and made himself so feared even by Andrea Doria that the Genoese despite favourable conditions twice refused to join battle with him.

Kheir-ed-Din died in 1547 and has his tomb in Istambul. But he got a worthy successor named Dragut Rais, whose courage was not broken even when Charles V in 1550 sent out a new naval expedition and captured Tripolis. Dragut attacked Capri in 1553, plundered the Certosa monastery and carried off many of the islanders as slaves. In letting the monastery's library and archives go up in flames, Dragut created in the long run a greater loss for the island than all of Kheir-ed-Din's raids.

The Capriotes constantly had to guard the island and its waters. The importance of this is seen in some rescripts from the royal Camera della Sommaria to the municipality of Capri in the 1560's concerning the latter's demand that those who lived in exile on the island should participate in guarding it and should also share the expenses for this task. Eight years later their request was granted, but was still a subject of contention in 1590.

The destruction caused by the pirates on Capri is evidenced by the lists of the island's population and *fuochi* (households) which together with many other documents were copied and in part published before they were destroyed in the Second World War. These lists show that the population decreased from 1,463 persons in 1523 to 1,093 in 1545.

In the 1560's, however, the Spanish viceroys began to take better care of Capri's defence by rebuilding the castles that Kheir-ed-Din razed and erecting new guard towers in addition to the two already existing, the one on Castiglione and the other one, built by the Certosa monks west of Anacapri, and now called Torre Materita. These castles, which still crown the peaks of Castiglione and Monte Solaro and the cliff above the « Phoenician Steps », as well as the towers on the slopes of Castiglione and Anacapri — Torre Materita, Torre Damecuta, Torre della Guardia — tell us of centuries of dread and are worth saving from decline and arbitrary restorations.

The first detailed description of Capri's topography and attractions is to be found in Fabio Giordano's Historia Napolitana, a work existing in a single manuscript, written in Latin in the second half of the 16th century and now preserved in the Biblioteca Nazionale in Naples. It has never been published in its entirety, probably because of its handwriting, which is very difficult to read. The chapter on Capri, however, has been published and annotated by Norman Douglas. A somewhat later description of the island, based in part on Giordano's work, is the Historia Neapolitana by Giulio Cesare Capaccio, first published in Naples in 1607. Among other things, Capaccio says that the inhabitants of the two communities Capri and Anacapri were enemies, lived in extreme poverty and were constantly exposed to attack by the Turkish pirates when fishing and sailing.

The great threat from the Turks was eliminated after their defeat against the united fleets of the Christian states in the sea battle at Lepanto in 1571 and by Vienna's being relieved from their siege in 1683. But the pirates of the Barbary states continued to make sailing unsafe in the Mediterranean for the next one hundred and fifty years. As late as 1826, according to Waiblinger, people on Capri still lived in dread of these pirates. Not until France captured the Barbary states in 1830 was their horrid activity brought to a definitive halt.

The history of Capri in the 17th century is characterized to a great extent by conflicts between clerical and secular authorities and internally within their ranks. The Bishops on the island sent petitions to the Holy See and to the Viceroys in Naples with complaints against the King's capitano, against the grasping and power-hungry monks of the Certosa monastery, about the fishing rights and fees and the tithes of the quail catch which they were entitled to collect. The quails were caught in nets, probably since antiquity, at the time of their spring and autumn migrations, when they flew in great flocks over the low central part of the island, where the place called Le Parate, « The Nets », still reminds one of this catch. Fabio Giordano mentions particularly the catch in the autumn, when the birds were at their fattest, saying that people usually salted what they could not finish fresh. The Bishop's tithes of the quail catch was an important and carefully guarded supplement to his scant wages; and for this reason, he was often derisively called *Il vescovo delle quaglie*, « the Quail Bishop ».

Strongly different from all this strife over worldly benefits are the life and work of the nun Suor Serafina. She is the great holy personage of Capri, even though the testimonies concerning her remarkable deeds were not considered sufficient for beatification, to say nothing of canonization. There is an enormous amount of handwritten material testifying to her life and works: about a hundred treatises and around two thousand letters of her own, two diaries kept by a pair of nuns between 1666 and 1689, other records kept by her relative Canon Ottavio Pisa and by a lawyer to one of her convents; and in

addition to all this, a biography written by the priest Don
Lutio Clemente. Based on these chronicles is the extensive
biography compiled by Pater N. Squillante, completed by Pater
T. Pagani, and printed in Naples in 1723. In modern times,
commendable studies on Suor Serafina have been published
by Norman Douglas and Edwin Cerio. A detailed and objective
biography of this remarkable woman cannot be written, however, before some competent person obtains the possibility of
examining and evaluating all the acts, including her letters and
treatises, of the beatification trial, the positive testimonies as
well as the negative ones proferred by the Advocatus Diaboli,
the « Devil's Advocate », all of which are now preserved in
the Santo Uffizio of the Vatican.

According to the evidence now available, whether true or
aimed to increase her honour, Suor Serafina in many ways
reflected the image of the great Spanish Saint, Teresa of Avila,
who died in 1582. She was born in Naples in 1621, the
daughter of a Neapolitan merchant, Nicolò Antonio Pisa, and
was baptized Prudenza. Her mother belonged to the old patrician Strina family of Capri, and the daughter therefore was
brought up at the foot of Castiglione, where a house is still
indicated as being *la casa di Suor Serafina*. From the age of
eight she experienced ecstasies, seeing Jesus in wondrous beauty
and hearing him talk to her as he would to his beloved bride.
She wrote letters and poems to her heavenly groom with ex-
pressions which, says Norman Douglas, an earthly Juliet could
direct to her Romeo. But she could not bear male children
near her, to say nothing of grown men or even her own father
— the only exception she made was for priests. Female physical functions were also repugnant to her. When her father
tried to force her to marry, she cut off her hair and announced
that she wanted to become a nun. She kept this decision even
though her father treated her badly — for which God sent
misfortunes upon him. She was a busy reader of St. Teresa's
writings and of tales about the lives of the martyrs. She fasted
and mortified her flesh in the most appalling ways, keeping

alive with the consecrated Host. When she was forced to bathe once she did it in scalding hot water. Only obedience to her Father Confessor's orders induced her to restrain her desire to humiliate her body. She was also visited by the Devil but did not yield to his temptations and once forced him to worship the Saviour. She even experienced the miracle of stigmatization, when the wounds of crucifixion appeared in her palms and a twelve-year old angel, perhaps Christ himself, pierced her heart with an arrow in the way illustrated by Bernini in his statue of St. Teresa in the church of Santa Maria della Vittoria in Rome. Like most holy men and women, she was said to have been able to cure the sick by touching them, to foresee the future, to float in the air, to appear at the same time in different places, to calm storms and volcanic eruptions, etc.

And like many other religious people, Suor Serafina combined ecstasy and ascetism, especially after she approached the age of fifty, with an imperative authority, a convincing eloquence, an indomitable will-power and a good understanding of how to deal with the realities of this world. She established a branch of the Carmelite order, whose strict rules, affined to those of St. Teresa, were dictated to her by the Virgin Mary and the Saviour himself. She began building her first convent on Capri from the small inheritance she had received from her mother and an uncle who had been her spiritual mentor, both of whom had died in the terrible plague which in 1656 decimated the population of the island. After a new revelation she got help from the Archbishop of Amalfi and the Viceroy in Naples, enabling the convent to be solemnly consacrated in 1678 by Cardinal Orsini, who as Pope Benedict XIII continued to support her. The convent was named in honour of St. Teresa and included the church of San Salvatore, consecrated in 1685, whose façade rises above Via Roma, the street leading from Due Mari onto the piazza of the town of Capri.

Between 1673 and 1691, Suor Serafina founded five other convents on the mainland and a sixth, the largest, in Anacapri, thereby fulfilling her promise to the Archangel Michael who, granting her prayers, rescued Vienna from the siege of the Turks. Remains of the last-mentioned convent are the walls which now enclose the Casa Timberina, behind the parish church of Santa Sofia, and the beautiful octagonal baroque church of San Michele, consecrated in 1719 and famous for its majolica floor representing Adam and Eve being expelled from the Garden of Eden (Fig. 28).

Suor Serafina's life was not one of self-willed suffering only. Her successes and influence earned her dangerous enmity from the Certosa monks and the Bishop of Capri, Paolo Pellegrino. The latter was an extremely quarrelsome prelate who with excommunication, interdicts and various affronts, and despite the fact that he was repeatedly suspended, persistently carried on feuds with the islanders, the Certosa monks, the Viceroys in Naples and their capitani on the island, even with the Archbishop in Amalfi and his own priests, whom he in vain tried to discipline by forbidding them to wear extravagant robes, to go hunting and fishing, to take part in drinking-bouts in the Grotta dei Preti, the « Cave of the Priests » on the east coast of the island, and to go swimming in the sea without underpants.

Suor Serafina was repeatedly accused before the Santo Uffizio in Rome of heresy, i.a. for having adopted the Spanish priest Miguel Molinos' quietistic doctrine, which won dangerously many and powerful followers: one of them, although not without strong reservations, was Queen Christina of Sweden, who in 1654 renounced the Swedish throne and shortly thereafter tried in vain to win the crown of Naples. Suor Serafina was accused, further, of witchcraft, necromancy, inebriation, falsehood and theft, for having had an incestuous relationship with her uncle and Father Confessor, and for having worn lace underwear. When she left her position as abbess, she was badly treated by her successor and had to witness how morality and order were dissolved in the convent she had founded. By order of the Inquisition she was locked up in a cell for two and a half years without even receiving Communion, until in 1691 a decree from the Santo Uffizio ordered her release, finding her not guilty of the sins of which she was accused. She regarded these and other trials as a favour from heaven in reply to her prayers asking to leave this world purified by sorrow, pain and abandonment. Her prayers were answered on March 17, 1699.

Her dead body did not get much repose either. Like the body of St. Teresa, we are told, it remained warm and pink, without stiffening and with no signs of decomposition, and it gave off an indescribably pleasant odour. Blood still coursed through her veins four days after her death, when her lungs, liver and kidneys were removed together with her intestines, to be inspected for signs which would strengthen the request of her being beatified. The extracted organs were put on exhibit five days later and viewed by an enormous number of people. The coffin containing her body was interred in the church of San Salvatore, but in 1813 it was moved to Santo Stefano, where it has been shifted three times and opened twice for investigation of the remains in connection with the drawnout beatification process. Since 1893, they repose under an inscribed plaque in the chapel to the right of the main altar.

Suddenly in the midst of this Capriote world of ecstatic piety, insidious intrigues by monks and priests, and terrible pirate outrages, there appeared an inquisitive and adventurous Frenchman named Jean Jacques Bouchard. This Bouchard travelled in Italy in the 1630's and carefully wrote down his impressions and experiences. His travel diary was found in 1850 at one of the bouquinistes on the banks of the Seine and was donated to the École des Beaux-Arts in Paris, where it is now preserved. It has been published by L. Marcheix, although only in excerpts and summaries. The chapter on Capri is reproduced in its entirety, however, even to the retention of Bouchard's somewhat irregular spelling, in Edwin Cerio's books entitled Capri nel Seicento and L'ora di Capri.

Bouchard called his father Agamemnon, his mother Cly-
temnestre and himself Orestes, which implies that his family
relationships were not particularly harmonic. He kept his eyes
open and acquired many valuable acquaintanceships during his
travels. After having stayed a while in Rome and Naples, he
visited Capri two days in May, 1632. He diligently took notes
and even made a scribbled little sketch of the island, which
caused him to be arrested as a spy on his way back in Salerno
by the suspicious Spaniards. He was taken to Naples and in-
carcerated in the Castel Nuovo with the prospect of being
hanged but was freed after a day or so, fortunately with his
papers intact and in his possession. He was the first tourist
on Capri, and his narration about what he saw and heard on
the island is so interesting and informative that the greater part
of it merits being reproduced here in translation.

« The inhabitants divide the island into two parts: towards the west is the mountain which they call *fuor di terra*
or Anna Capra's mountain; the part which lies to the east is
Capri proper. There is the old town, situated approximately
in the middle of the island on a plateau, a good half mille by
foot from the harbour. It looked quite nice from a distance,
with towers and crenellated walls, but once inside there are
only small streets so narrow that two persons can barely pass
each other. The houses are small, low, with only one storey
and completely round above, without a roof of either tile or
wood or thatch. They are merely plastered with pozzolana,
which is rather ugly, although the custom is I do not know
how old. There are only 150 inhabited houses, everything else
is deserted and half in ruin, and no more than about 700 souls
live there. Presently there is only one parish church, Santo Stefano, by the square; the two others which existed previously
are in disrepair, as are many other small chapels and churches, of which there are about seventy in the town and *four
di terra*. And the Bishop's deputy, of the old Curtis family,
said to Orestes that this large number of churches had been
built in the time of the French so that the women could hear

112

mass without having to go far from home and expose themselves to the impudence and insolence of that nation: a sly invention by the Spanish, who were clever enough to give a malicious interpretation to the Frenchmen's piety, which without a doubt gave rise to this number of churches. This town is ruled by a mayor, elected men and so-called *Catapani,* who are in charge of provisions, and who in Naples and other cities in Italy are called *quelli della grascia.* Furthermore there is the royal captain who rules the entire island but is forced to live in the town; he cannot even spend the night out of his house, cannot even go to Anna Capra and sleep there. Among other decrees, there is one of special note which says that no one may carry a stick or cane thicker than a finger and of certain length, under penalty of prison or fines. The castle, which is situated on a high mountain, is impregnable, according to the natives, because in addition to its high and steep location, there is a big cave in the middle of the mountain which the besieged can reach by means of ladders, removing themselves without fear of being overpowered, as they have a rock 20 toises (close to 40 yards) around them.

The other part, Anna Crapa, is not called a town though it has 200 households and 800 souls, but *terra,* since it is not surrounded by walls and the houses are built haphazardly without ordered streets and rather far from each other. The origin of the name Anna Crapa is controversial. The islanders themselves say that a goat, climbing up the mountain that the community rests on, first showed the way thither, which did not exist before this and truthfully seems to be made for goats, as steep and full of precipices as it is, in addition to the fact that in order to reach the top, one must climb up 700 steps carved out of the cliff two or three hundred years ago. Up here one has one of the most beautiful views in Italy. And thus they say that a man who was tending the goat and saw it climb, followed it and said *Anna Crapa,* which in the local dialect means *anda capra,* that is « go goat », and when they arrived up on the top, they built the town there. But the learned men say that the orginal town was down by the harbour before, on the place where the Bishop's mansion still is today, which has been damaged by pirates, particularly Saracens. The people then took to the mountains where they were more secure, and some settled down where the town now stands and others where the « countryside » is, and they started to build with the agreement that the two communities should be one, even though they were separate. Therefore they put the particle *ana* onto the latter, which pharmacists use even today for their prescriptions in the sense of *simul et aequaliter*. In the second book of his Latin history, Capacius says that this *ana* is a distorted ανϖ, that is « Capri up there », which is probable.

The inhabitants of these two communities hate each other passionately, and in general these islanders are very nasty, quarrelsome, defiant, thieving, and arrogant, and they all die of hunger. They are good sailors and build excellent boats, and the majority of the men who work at the arsenal in Naples come from this island. And Capacius says that since they are thus detained in Naples in the service of the King, and therefore anxious about their womenfolk, who are very beautiful, as are the young boys, they have obtained as a favour that those who have been exiled to Capri by the Viceroys are not allowed to stay overnight in Anna Crapa; Orestes was assured that both the women and the young boys greatly enjoy love making. The women raise a large number of silk worms which are called *agnolelle* because they are so beautiful. The silk from this island is the most highly valued of all the silk coming from Italy.

The parish church in Anna Crapa is called Santa Sophia, which indicates that the island was inhabited by Greeks previously, as does an insult which they use, calling each other Albanians to express their censure and contempt. When Orestes rested in the confessional chair in this church, he read a list of restrictions, among other things that all parents who allow brothers and male cousins to sleep in the same bed as their

sisters and female cousins when they were over seven years
old should be excommunicated.

The silk island has an abundance of olive groves, vineyards, orchards, wheat, flax and vegetables on the lower
sections towards the harbour. The mountains are covered with
oaks, holly, laurel, barberry bushes, myrtle, rosemary, etc. The
greatest share of all this goes to the Carthusian monks, who
have a monastery there, rather fine and fortified, since it has a
sturdy tower with artillery and other weapons for defence
against the Turks. Its church is pretty and the cells very pleasant, for example the one which is inhabited by an old monk
well versed in mathematics who has hewn out over fifty steps
from the cliff and made diverse rooms and passages in it. He
has also carved out more than one hundred steps from the same
cliff which lead all the way down to the sea. He has done all
this with his own hands, and without the help of anyone else.
He had devoted over thirty years of his life to this task, and
three days after Orestes had departed from Capri, he heard it
said that the poor man of God, who had one foot in the grave,
had been chased out of his cell and arbitrarily sent to Naples.
The usual kindness of monks. Orestes stayed with them and
was very well entertained. Among other things he ate a kind
of small *ricotte,* made of goat milk, which are so extraordinary
that they are sent as presents to all of Naples' gentlemen. The
monastery's income reaches 15,000 écus, while that of the bi-
shopric hardly amounts to 300; and this income furthermore
is uncertain, because if the quails on their way back from Egypt
in the springtime come in large flocks and rest on the island,
which they do almost every spring, the Bishop can feast, if
not, his income stops at 100 or 200 écus. And that is why he
is called *il Vescovo delle Quaglie.* Because of this, the Bishop's
mansion is quite delapidated, and there is not a village church
in France which is not in better condition.

The local people believe that the body of San Costanzo
is there, but they do not dig at the place, and even worse, they
will not dig, because they are afraid that if other people should

find out, he will be taken from them. And it is no use asking
them where he is, for then they will believe that you have
come only to carry him away. The wines of this island are good,
mainly white and light, rather tasty but a little sour. The island
also produces Greek wine, which is well liked.

Today the island is a place of punishment to which the
viceroys generally exile those lords of the Kingdom who have
committed crimes, while in times past the Roman Emperors
preferred it to the rest of the world that they ruled, and purchased it in order to spend a large part of their lives on it.
Fate, not satisfied with having ruined and changed the entire
beatiful countryside between Rome and Naples, has also vent-
ed its anger upon the smallest islands. Nevertheless, this island
has preserved many important remains of its ancient prosperity in the many *anticaglie,* which even today as ruins beat
the most impressive buildings you can find to admire in Naples.
There are four of them which are particularly worthy of note.
One of them lies high up on the top of the mountain which
forms the corner of the island towards the cape of Massa. It
could well have been Tiberius' palace, the Villa Jovis, which
was the most beautiful of the twelve villas and was also called
« the Fortress » by Pliny, both because of its size, having three
storeys with porticos, one above the other, and because it
was situated on the edge of a precipice from which, according
to Suetonius, he took great pleasure in having people thrown
off. The second *anticaglia* is on Monte Sant'Angelo approximately in the middle of the island, and it is very big. The other
two lie near the sea by the foot of the mountain which leads
up to Anna Crapa and faces Naples; the one is now called Tragara and the other, Il Palazzo. The inhabitants say that the
Emperors held these four palaces for the four seasons and that
they had a large road built to enable them to travel by carriage
from one villa to another, and they point out traces of it
which still survive today. They have yet another tradition
which says that after Tiberius' death, the Romans sent five
hundred masons to the island who during a period of six months

116

tore down and destroyed these beautiful buildings to prevent other Emperors from leaving Rome and settling down here.

In addition to these four villas, the island is full of other *anticaglie,* one of which is particularly beautiful. It is situated towards the western point below Anna Capra and is called the Grotto, being a large cave under the island, with the opening facing south. They call it *La grotta scura,* since on entering it one sees nothing; then one gradually begins to see the sea, which rushes into the cave, and several rivulets which drip down above. Capacius seems to reckon it among the things that the Romans constructed on the island, but the Carthusians assured Orestes that it was a cave which had been carved out of the rock by natural means. Orestes could not come into it, because the entrance was very low and the sea was rough and stormy just then ».

Bouchard, his countryman Montaigne, and the Englishmen Fynes Moryson, Thomas Coryat, George Sandys, and John Evelyn, belong to the small group of foreign travellers who visited Italy during the late 16th and the early 17th centuries and described their experiences there. Bouchard, however, was the only one of them who ventured to cross over to Capri. Sandys, who on his return voyage from Palestine and Egypt sailed along the coast of Calabria towards Naples, gives a description of Capri in his Relation of a Iourney begun An: Dom: 1610, but he was satisfied in writing down what he had read in Capaccio, without bothering to set foot on the island himself.

In his description of Capri, Bouchard appears as a somewhat chauvinistic Frenchman, convinced of the excellence of his country and countrymen, critical of the islanders and, no doubt with justice, of the Spanish rulers. He must therefore be read with a grain of salt. The picture he paints of the decline and depopulation of the island due to the ravages of the pirates is undoubtedly correct. His report about the animosity between the two communities Capri and Anacapri is confirmed by many similar statements, from the Middle Ages

and the 15th century to Capaccio and later (cf. above, pp. 97,
106, 114). He has no sensitivity for what the 19th and 20th
century tourists have found so pretty and picturesque: the
narrow medieval streets and the peculiar architecture, which
has preserved up to the present day the types of barrel vault
inherited from the late Roman and Byzantine periods, simple,
crossed, or changed into square low pseudo-cupolas. An architecture which has often been rashly attributed to the Saracens
— as if on Capri and other places in southern Italy, one
learned how to build houses from the marauding pirates! The
fact that he misses ordinary roofs covered with tiles, shingles
or thatch (!), and that he finds the gray plaster of the houses
ugly, shows his lack of understanding of the influence of the
climate on architecture and his lack of knowledge concerning
plastering with gray pozzolana mortar, which resists wind and
weather better than the whitewash used nowadays. His conclusion that the name of the church of Santa Sofia implies
that the island was once inhabited by Greeks is right in so
far as this name — like so many others: San Costanzo, San
Michele, Santa Maria di Costantinopoli, San Bartolomeo de
Romeis — gives evidence for the Byzantine influence on Capri.
His degrading opinion of the islanders, their behaviour and
their sexual habits (in a copy of his notes, he calls the lovely
women of Capri *puttane,* harlots) must, like all other gene-
ralisations, be taken *cum grano salis.* His sarcasm towards
monks in general, *gentillesse ordinaire des moines,* seems
unfair since he was given room and excellent board in the
Certosa monastery.

Clearly he viewed the ruins of the imperial palaces with
admiration, even though he refers to them in the derogatory
term common to simple folk in Italy, and which he no doubt
heard from his ciceroni: *anticaglie,* « old rubbish ». His indication that the Villa Jovis was up to three storeys high, with
porticos one above the other, shows that the ruin was much
better preserved in his time than now. He probably also visited
the ruins on Monte San Michele, also called Monte Sant'An-

gelo, as well as those named Palazzo a Mare and Bagni di Tiberio. These latter ruins are probably what he erroneously calls Tragara, perhaps confusing this name with the nearby Punta Trasete. The remains of an ancient road which he was shown most likely was the series of arches which was called *Le Camerelle* and imagined to have been Tiberius' *sellaria* (cf. above, p. 56).

He supplemented his own observations with what he had heard from the islanders and what he had read in his Capaccio, whose work was the Baedeker of the time for Naples and its surroundings. The local people fed him some fanciful tales, typical for the speculations of half-literates, about how the communities Capri and Anacapri originated, how Anacapri got its name and what it meant, how old the ancient steps leading up there could be, and why the imperial villas were so badly destroyed. The statement that there had been 70 churches and chapels on the island probably was exaggerated; a list of the names of all the churches, extant or only mentioned in documents, shows that in the 17th century there were hardly more than about fifty, which is quite a large number for an island of Capri's size. Most of them do not exist any more.

Bouchard frequently cites Capaccio and like Sandys takes his description of the Grotta Oscura from him; but he admits honestly that he did not succeed in entering the cave because of the weather. All the same, during his two days on Capri, he gathered more facts about the island than most of its later short-time visitors have done.

CAPRI UNDER THE BOURBONS

After the Spanish king Philip V of Bourbon, five kings of the same house ruled over the kingdoms of Naples and Sicily, from 1734 to 1860, when Garibaldi captured Sicily and took over in Naples. The longest reign was that of the infantile and completely uneducated Ferdinand IV (1759-1825). He was forced two times, however, to abandon the throne of Naples and flee to Palermo, once for several months during the short-lived Parthenopean Republic (1799) and once for nine years, when Napoleon's brother Joseph Bonaparte and his brother-in-law Joachim Murat ruled in Naples (1806-1815).

The reign of the Bourbons was characterized by misrule, hard punishment of all « liberals », and an amazing ability to thwart all attempts to create a representative assembly. Large sums were set aside for the construction of the impressive royal palaces in Caserta, in Portici and on Capodimonte in Naples. Court etiquette was stilted and complicated in the Spanish way. On the plus side can be noted the creation of a navy which won several victories over the pirates from the Barbary states, the founding of Naples' celebrated opera, Teatro San Carlo, and the establishment of the Museo Archeologico in the large 16th century palace which still houses its unique collections. This museum received the antiques from Herculaneum, Pompeii and Stabiae which had been kept in the royal palace in Portici. The excavations in the buried towns, discovered in the 1730's and 40's, were conducted without plan and method, with many interruptions and exclusively for the purpose of finding sculptures, paintings, mosaics and other valuable objects. The finds were considered as royal property, jealously guarded and disposed of in accordance with royal whims. Lady

M. W. Montagu, a prominent Englishwoman on a six-week visit to Naples in the beginning of the 1740's, narrates in her Letters from France and Italy that she spent a large part of that time attempting in vain to get permission to visit the palace in Portici in order to see the finds from Herculaneum. She also recounts that a beautiful bronze statue of a Vestal, found at Herculaneum, was melted down to make memorial medaillons for the christening of one of the many royal babies.

Of the five Bourbon kings, only Charles, who became Charles III of Spain in 1759, and his son Ferdinand IV seem to have shown any interest in Capri. Charles instructed the governor of the island, Giuseppe Maria Secondo, to make an inventory of its remains of ancient monuments, certainly for the purpose of insuring a supply of marble for the construction of the palace in Caserta. He appropriated the entire 1750 edition of Secondo's printed reports, probably to safeguard himself against any possible rivals in the field of marble-searching. Fortunately, however, this important work was reprinted in A.F. Gori's Symbolae, of 1752, and was reissued in 1808, lacking only the dedication to the King, the occasional use of the word *Sire,* and a few lines at the end. Ferdinand released the islanders from active service, gave them a civil governor instead of the previous military one, persuaded them to set up a force of armed citizens as a protection against the pirates, and visited the island very often, to hunt quail. His interest in its ancient remains was limited, however, to his giving Norbert Hadrawa permission to conduct his destructive excavations and to securing for himself those ancient sculptures, columns and marble floors that could be of use in his palaces.

From the middle of the 17th century, Italy had become the goal for an everincreasing number of travellers, in particular Englishmen, Germans and Frenchmen, making the Grand Tour of Europe. They were primarily authors and scholars, with a young nobleman every now and then, who guided by his tutor, gained necessary education in this way. Information for the travellers was supplied by books such as Misson's

Nouveau voyage d'Italie (1691-98) and Volkmann's Nachrichten von Italien (1770-71).

Of all these travellers, however, there were but a very few who went further south than Naples and perhaps, like Gustavus III of Sweden in 1784, got permission to visit the excavations in Pompeii and Herculaneum, and even fewer still who braved the sea and threat of pirates to cross over to Capri. K. Ph. Moritz says in his book entitled Reisen eines Deutschen in Italien in den Jahren 1786-1788 (Berlin 1792) that during Ferdinand IV's hunting expeditions to Capri, two armed ships continually cruised around the island to prevent the possibility of the King's being seized by pirates from Tripolis.

One of those courageous few was Joseph Addison, famous for his satirical descriptions of contemporary life in The Tatler, The Spectator and The Guardian. In his Remarks on Several Parts of Italy, etc. in the Years 1701, 1702, 1703, Addison tells about his visit to the Grotta Oscura, already described by Giordano and Capaccio, which at that time was considered one of the island's major attractions. Another famous 18th century traveller who dared cross over to Capri was Montesquieu, who visited the island in 1729 and, like his countryman Bouchard almost a century before, enjoyed the hospitality of the Certosa monks, according to what he says in his Voyages (Bordeaux 1894-96). Montesquieu heard the same story about the destruction of the imperial villas that was told to Bouchard, but otherwise has much less to tell about the island.

For seventeen years around the middle of the 18th century, Capri was the scene of the activities of the English Baronet Sir Nathaniel Thorold. Sir Nathaniel is the first of the numerous foreigners who have remained on the island until their death. His life and deeds constitute an important chapter in the history of economy, interlarded with many hilarious, picant and macabre happenings. All of these are described by Edwin Cerio on the basis of English genealogies, Capriote church books, wills, court proceedings and other documents, supplemented by the narration of an old Capriote which is recorded in a diary kept by a Scottish doctor, George Sidney Smith Clark. Dr. Clark lived on the island in the 19th century and, according to a memorial plaque in the town hall of Capri, greatly aided the sick and the poor; he died in 1868 and is buried in the cemetery of Anacapri. Copies of the documents are kept in the library of the Centro Caprense. The statements made in them are not always consistent, but the main features in the Baronet's notable life can clearly be described.

To avoid being imprisoned for unpaid debts, Sir Nathaniel fled to Holland from his ancestral home in Harmston, Lincolnshire. While in Holland, he met a fellow countryman in exactly the same precarious situation. To save himself, the latter had come upon the brilliant idea that the big cod fish which, as hard-dried stock-fish or split-cod, had been an important element in the northeners' diet for centuries, could become a suitable item, if slightly dried and salted, for the Catholics' meat-free Fridays and, therefore, a profitable export to southern countries. The two paupers decided to go in together on the project. Dr. Clark's source does not mention how it was financed, but it is certain that Sir Nathaniel safely landed in Genoa with the first cargo of cured cod, which the Italians call *baccalà,* and made a good profit. After a while he moved his baccalà business to Livorno, where he became a rich man. Ever since, *baccalà alla livornese,* soaked and cooked with onions, tomatoes, olive oil and spices, has been an inexpensive and delicious Friday dish in all of Italy and still is in those homes and trattorias that keep alive the tradition.

In Livorno Sir Nathaniel rented quarters from a pharmacist named Antonino Canale and soon became a friend of the family. Canale at the age of about seventy had married Anna della Noce, the most beautiful girl in the city and fifty years his junior. The unavoidable love affair between the lovely Anna and the English nobleman quickly caused offence and led to persecution from the church authorities, even though the spouse in real or pretended blindness swore to his wife's faithfulness and his friend's innocence. Because of all this, the Englishman moved to Naples with his mistress, his pharmacist and his baccalà, and continued there with his flourishing business. When, however, his *ménage à trois* created problems in Naples as well, he moved with the whole household over to Capri. In this way, the cured cod fish import to Italy came to be directed from this island for seventeen years.

On Capri, Sir Nathaniel bought a house near Due Mari which once belonged to the 17th century Bishop Gallo. The house, renovated and impressively enlarged, and decorated with frescoes, the Baronet's coat-of-arms and English furniture, became generally known as the Palazzo Inglese. Here the idyll between Sir Nathaniel and Anna bloomed and resulted in a multitude of children who were all given the family name Canale, and who sweetened the kind pharmacist's old age. Naturally, this peculiar family was the source of gossip even on Capri, but the only one who seemed to be really worried about the sinful life at the Palazzo Inglese was Monsignor Rocco, the Bishop of the island. When Sir Nathaniel continued to live together with Anna after the pharmacist died, thus making it impossible for even the most credulous to consider him as just a friend of the family, the Bishop felt called upon to report this *scandalum* in solemn Latin to the Holy See in 1754, telling also how he had tried in vain to force the two sinners to separate. When no Papal intervention was forthcoming, he tried instead to get the Baronet to marry Anna. The Englishman never refused, but he constantly put off the matter with a polite « by and by ». These words were repeated so often that they became a current expression on Capri for something which is protracted indefinitely: *Baibai dicette 'u 'nglese.*

The pious Bishop also did his best to try to convert Sir Nathaniel to the Catholic faith. But his persuasions were always countered by the sinful heretic with one of the few

Italian words he had learnt, the much-used and useful *pazienza*. And when a friend urged him to think about his death and make his will, he met with the same request to have patience: *Pazienza!*

When Sir Nathaniel lay on his death bed in 1764, Anna and his friends believed that they could make out in the mumble of words he uttered his surrender to their prayers and his desire to take Holy Communion like a good Catholic. The Bishop was summoned and came in procession with the priests from the Cathedral. But in reply to all of his prayers, questions and encouragements, the dying man said only *Pazienza,* repeating this word for several hours, right up to his death. Since he had thus avoided becoming a Catholic up to the very end, he was not buried in consecrated ground but in a near-by vineyard.

Poor Anna, now twice a widow, had to face the fact that she was unable to inherit the wealth of her children's father, since he had not bothered to legalize their relationship nor, apparently, to leave a will. But she was by no means at a loss. She summoned a shrewd clerk named Michele Pagano, who without trembling wrote out a document in his most elegant bureaucratic Italian, in which he certified that Sir Nathaniel Thorold, bed-ridden and bodily weak but, through the grace of God, of sound mind, clear in speech and thought, and able to both understand and speak Italian, considering the frailty and caducity of human nature and the fact that nothing is more certain than death and nothing more uncertain than the hour in which it arrives — *considerando lo stato fragile e caduco dell'umana natura, e che non c'è cosa più certa della Morte, e niuna più incerta dell'ora di quella,* says the original text — had bidden him to make out this will by which he leaves all his worldy possessions (specified in full detail) to Anna della Noce.

Unfortunately for Anna, two authentic vills were found later, one which had been left with Sir Nathaniel's partners in Naples for safe-keeping, and one which he had made during his last visit to Harmston, in which he appointed Anna della Noce's first-born son Samuele as heir to the land and title and stated that he himself should be buried in England. Several years of litigation resulted in the heir, still a minor, being placed under the legal guardianship of no other than England's Lord Chancellor, who sent out a ship to fetch the youth and the Baronet's remains.

Now, however, it was learned that the two who had taken care of Sir Nathaniel's burial had also passed away, and that no one could find the site of the grave. But Anna, not wanting to cross someone as important as the Lord Chancellor of England, once again came up with a solution. She had the remains of an old hermit who had died at about the same time as Sir Nathaniel dug up and shipped to England, where they were placed in a sarcophagus and entombed in the Thorold family vault in Harmston. Samuele Canale also arrived in England and as Sir Samuel in due time took over his father's property and family name. The only thing more that is known of Anna della Noce is the notation that she died in 1787, the widow of the deceased Antonino Canale.

The Palazzo Inglese according to some was also willed to Samuele, according to others, to his brother Natale. In any case, it remained in the possession of the family and is described by Hadrawa as the most beautiful house on Capri, where King Ferdinand and all of his retinue used to live during the quail hunts. During the almost two and a half years that Capri was in the hands of the English, the Palazzo was the residence of Hudson Lowe and for this reason was badly damaged by cannon fire when the French captured the island in October of 1808 (below, p. 133). The house still exists, though in a state of dilapidation.

Between the years 1781 and 1786, the French Abbé J.C. de Saint-Non published his monumental work entitled Voyage pittoresque ou Description des royaumes de Naples et de Sicile, richly illustrated with engravings made after drawings sketched by a staff of travelling French artists. Among these engravings there are two made by J. de Longueil after drawings by C.L. Chatelet, showing Capri seen from the north and from the east; the artist, or more likely the engraver, has taken the license of making the cliffs look more rugged than they do in reality. Another of Saint-Non's assistants was Jean Desprez, who later was employed by Gustavus III of Sweden and was active in this country until his death in 1804. During his travels in Sicily and southern Italy in 1777-79, Desprez made a number of drawings on Capri, known to us, however, only through his later compositions. Among the latter is a sepia-tinted drawing now in the National Museum in Stockholm, depicting « The Roman Emperor Tiberius having exiles thrown from a cliff on the island of Capri ». The drawing, probably based on a sketch made on the spot, shows the precipice of Monte Tiberio crowned by a reconstructed Villa Jovis and peopled down its sides by spear-bearing soldiers.

In May 1787, the great Goethe, returning from Sicily to Naples aboard a French merchant vessel, was almost shipwrecked on Capri's rocks. Twenty-nine years later he describes the adventure in his Italienische Reise, sparing no dramatic effect: how the becalmed ship is drawn by the current closer and closer to the threatening cliffs as night is falling, how the women cry to the saints and the men complain to the captain about bad food and bad seamanship, how he himself comes forth and gives an encouraging speech, comparing their situation with that of the terror-stricken apostles on the Sea of Tiberias, how the sailors put a rowboat into the sea and with it try in vain to hold the ship against the current, how some goatherds come into view around their fires up on the cliffs, emitting hoarse yells which the imperiled passengers interpret as shouts of joy at the prospect of all the goods which would be washed ashore after the wreck — and how just then, the sails fill and carry the vessel away from the dangerous island. The next morning, Goethe viewed Capri with satisfaction from a comforting distance.

One of Goethe's contemporaries, Count Friedrich Leopold von Stolberg, came to Capri five years later and participated in one of Hadrawa's excavations in the Grotta di Matromania, which he describes in his Reise durch Deutschland, die Schweiz, Italien und Sizilien, published in 1794. It was just during these years, from 1786 to 1804, that Hadrawa carried out his destructive excavations in the ruins of Capri's imperial villas, praised by Ambassador Hamilton and all the others who saw the chance of enriching their collections with objects given or sold by the shrewd diplomat and antique dealer. Particularly pleased was of course King Ferdinand, since he got the lion's share of columns and marble floors. The King, according to Hadrawa's vivid description, was also present at one of the excavations, when the men and women of the digging team after finishing a successful treasure hunt made the King's favourite dish of spaghetti, which were eaten with the fingers in the Neapolitan way, after which they danced the tarantella among the ruins of the imperial villa.

Hadrawa, however, gives not only accounts of his excavations, but also interesting descriptions of how people lived on the island at the end of the 18th century. He states that the town of Capri about 1790 had 2.000 inhabitants, while Anacapri had 1.300, that the two communities lived in enmity, and that people in Anacapri were more honest than those in Capri: a judgement which may at least in part be due to the fact that he conducted his excavations only in Capri's section of the island and there experienced some unpleasant behaviour of his workers. The chief products of the island, wine, olive oil, fruit, fish, and cheese, were taken by boat to Naples two times a week, occasionally to other sites around the Bay as well. Quail hunting was still profitable: Hadrawa gives the number af 12.000 as the record catch for one day. Many men were engaged in coral fishing off Sardinia the whole summer and did not return home before the autumn — apart from those who were seized by pirates and never returned. Among their many other privileges, the Certosa monks could keep goats and lived a sumptuous life; they baked the best bread on the island, produced and sold a famous liqueur, but in times of need, handed out flour, bread and other food. There was no inn on the island: strangers usually took any food they might need with them and applied for lodging with the governor or at the Palazzo Inglese. The only time that meat was available was when a cow fell down a precipice and died: in that case, a trumpet was blown as the signal that meat was for sale in the piazza.

Five years after Hadrawa published his Ragguagli, a little book entitled Fragmente über Italien aus dem Tagebuch eines jungen Deutschen came out in Germany. For some reason, it lacks the name of the author and that of the publishing site. The former, however, is shown to have been a German newspaper man named Carl Joseph Stegmann. He stayed on the island for three days in 1797 and seems to have used this short time with German efficiency. His descriptions of what he saw confirm and supplement Hadrawa's information. He lived in the governor's house near Due Mari, went on a quail hunt and visited the two monasteries. He seems to have been greeted less cordially by the Certosa monks because of his critical comments about their goats, who damaged both the woods and agriculture. According to Stegmann, the most important products of the island were wine and olive oil, both highly prized but produced in far too limited quantities due to the barren soil. Extensive cattle-breeding allowed the islanders to conduct a fairly large trade in calves, butter and cheese. The money they made, however, went partly towards the purchase of manufactured articles, grain and garden products which the island could not produce in sufficient quantities, partly, and primarily, towards the paying of fees to the Bishop, the cathedral chapter and the two monasteries, which owned almost all of the cultivated land on the island and oppressed the inhabitants with requests of work, rents and tithes.

Stegmann states that in 1797 the town of Capri had 2.070 inhabitants, Anacapri 1.544. Like Hadrawa, he finds that the people in Anacapri differ positively from the rest of the inhabitants: they were taller, more wiry, less dark and more like northern Italians. The differences in character were as great: it was said that in Anacapri many years could pass without one hearing of a child born out of wedlock, court proceedings were almost as rare, and the fact that no house there had a lock on the door was a good indication that thievery was also something unusual.

Stegmann also states, with a hint of approval, that Hadrawa continued his excavations despite opposition from the chapter and the monasteries. He even tells us what Hadrawa had left of his finds in 1797, after the best of them had already been disposed of, and his prizes. There were mainly capitals, columns and marble floors on the price list, plus « a bust of Agrippina, and another one of a child, somewhat damaged. 20 Ducats ».

Stegmann also met the Bishop of Capri, Monsignor Nicola Saverio Gamboni, whom he describes as « anything but malevolent, but so involved in the intrigues of the high clergy that he rarely gets a few minutes extra to think about his flock's spiritual, to say nothing of its physical well-being ». This jugement is not untrue, but greatly exaggerated. A memorial plaque on a building near the Palazzo Cerio recalls even today the seminary that was founded there by Gamboni, who also started four schools for male students, with instruction among other things in agriculture and seamanship, and a school for girls, with teaching in reading, writing and silk weaving. But he seems to have been an opportunist who knew how to get along even when he supported the wrong side. Faced with the advancing French army, Ferdinand IV, who in 1798 joined the coalition against France, fled to Sicily with Queen Maria Carolina, Ambassador Hamilton and his lovely Lady Emma on board one of Nelson's warships. In the meantime, the liberals in Naples under the protection of the French proclaimed

130

the Parthenopean Republic. Gamboni in his sermons sided with
the Republicans. But when after six months Naples capitulated
to Cardinal Fabrizio Ruffo's army of ruffians and farmers, and
Ferdinand returned under the protection of Nelson's fleet,
things looked bad for the Bishop and the rebels. Admiral
Francesco Caracciolo was hanged as a traitor, and many others
shared his fate. Among them was also Dr. Gennaro Arcucci
from Capri, in spite of his having presented the King with
the Mithras relief (p. 65) and written a Relazione al Re sulle
antichità di Capri (1790): according to a memorial plaque in
the piazza of Capri, he was executed March 18, 1800. Gamboni, on the other hand, got off with banishment, departed
and succeeded in cultivating Napoleon's favour to such an
extent that he ended as Patriarch of Venice, dying there in
1808. He was the last Bishop of Capri.

When King Ferdinand had to flee to Sicily for the second
time to escape Napoleon's troups under Massena, who in
January 1806 took Naples, Capri too was occupied by the
French. But as early as May of the same year, an English fleet
put troops ashore near Marina Grande who under the command
of Sir W. Sidney Smith forced the French, despite gallant resistance, to capitulate. Colonel Hudson Lowe was installed as
military governor of the island, taking his head-quarters in the
Palazzo Inglese. Relatively undisturbed for the next two years,
he had Captain Richard Church to carry out the fortification
work which turned Capri into a « Little Gibraltar » and caused
irreparable damage to the ruins of the imperial villas. Lowe
also made the island a centre for the agents and propagandists
plotting the death of Joseph Bonaparte in order to effectuate
the return of the King and Queen.

After two unsuccessful attacks against the island during
the reign of Joseph Bonaparte, his successor, Joachim Murat,
shortly after acceding to the throne, decided to make a strong
effort to remove the threat against Naples that this « Little
Gibraltar » constituted. The operation was planned with great
care and secrecy so as to be able to start on a day when the

sea was calm and no English warships were about. Murat's
Chief of Police, a Corsican named Cristoforo Saliceti, also managed to get hold of one of Hudson Lowe's spies who happened
to be another Corsican, and by suitable means of persuasion
convinced his countryman to be a double agent. He carried
out this task with great dexterity, i.a. with the help of forged
letters in which Queen Maria Carolina complained about Lowe
and Lowe about the Queen. Another of Saliceti's spies was
Pietro Colletta, an Italian, who disguised as a fisherman re-
connoitered landing sites on Capri and made a plan of operation. He also participated in the landing, gradually became
a general, and in his Relazione della Conquista di Capri described the events.

The invasion was set into motion October 4, 1808, under
the command of General Jean Maximin Lamarque. While two
French-Neapolitan flottillas under heavy cannon-fire made mock
attacks against Marina Grande and Marina Piccola, causing
Hudson Lowe to concentrate the defence around these two natural landing places, the real attack was directed towards the
west coast of the island. There, despite fire from the forts that
the English had built at Punta Pino, Campetiello and Orrico, the
landing troops managed to force the heights with the help of
ladders and threw the defenders, the Royal Maltese Regiment,
from their positions. Creating a pincer movement with the help
of other French troops who had landed at Grotta Gradola, the
invaders forced the Maltese troops to retreat towards Monte
Solaro. Two Corsican companies which Hudson Lowe had sent
as relief from the town of Capri were also driven back, ma-
naging to escape down the « Phoenician Steps », the same way
they had come, while a third Corsican company under the command of Captain Church had to make a dangerous retreat
during the night along Il Passatiello, the path leading down
the steep east side of Monte Santa Maria. The Maltese capitulated and were taken as prisoners to Naples. Their commander, an Irish major named John Hamill, had been killed; thirty
years later his remains were brought by relatives to the ceme-

tery of Anacapri, where his grave is marked by a memorial plaque.

The French now controlled Anacapri and directed their fire from its heights towards the town of Capri, with the Palazzo Inglese as one of their special targets, as Hudson Lowe had his quarters there. He returned fire from Castiglione and Monte San Michele, but despite this, the French managed to get down the ancient steps to Campo Pisco. Then the situation came to more or less of a standstill: faced with the risk of incurring a loss by storming the fortified town, the French hesitated, while Hudson Lowe remained inside the walls in anticipation of the arrival of the English fleet. Joachim Murat came personally to Massa on the Sorrento Peninsula to see how it all would end.

At last a Sicilian-British fleet showed up, but due to bad weather, it either could not or did not dare bring help to the besieged. Whereas French supply ships sailed across to the island, escorted by cannon boats making sallies against the enemy vessels. These cruised around for a few day off Capri, then disappeared. At this point, Hudson Lowe surrendered, on October 17th. He was treated honourably, and was allowed to leave the island together with his troops on their own ships and sail to Sicily: a decision which Napoleon is said to have disapproved of strongly. The same day that the terms of surrender were signed, a large English fleet, composed of warships and transport vessels, came into view to rescue Capri — just a few hours too late. Hudson Lowe must have left Capri in bitterness. Eight years later he found himself governor of another small island, St Helena, where Napoleon lived for six years as a prisoner. Both the guardian and the guarded seem to have taken advantage of any and all opportunities to make life difficult for the other.

The capture of « Little Gibraltar » is described by Sir Hudson Lowe himself in his private papers, now kept at the British Museum, by Pietro Colletta and other eye-witnesses, and later on by scholars such as Sir Lees Knowles, M. Perrot,

P. Pieri and E. Simion. The event was also immortalized by French and Italian poets in the high-flown, grandiloquent language of the era. The most interesting of these last-mentioned works is an epic poem in twelve cantos which was published in Naples in 1892, entitled *La Presa di Capri*, by Francesco Alberino. This Alberino was a Capriote carpenter who was born the same year that Capri was captured. In a collection of verses called Anacapri civilizzato, published posthumously in 1902, he is presented as *poeta estemporaneo ed illetterato,* « an extemporizing and illiterate poet ». Since La Presa di Capri seems to have been written by an eye-witness and possesses literary merit (according to Norman Douglas, it is reminiscent of no less a poet than William Blake), and since a handwritten fragment of the poem has comments made most likely by a priest named Antonio Farace, Edwin Cerio is probably right in his supposition that the real author was not the carpenter-improvisator Alberino but this priest, who possibly heard the events narrated by an uncle who owned the house where Major Hamill lived.

The capture was immortalized also in two monumental paintings by the Neapolitan artist Odoardo Fischetti which now are to be seen in the Museo Nazionale di San Martino in Naples. One of them shows the French landing on the west coast of Capri, with ladders and other equippment (Fig. 29), the other, Murat with his offcers in the neighbourhood of Massa, in heroic position (Fig. 30).

Shortly after the capture of Capri, on the 12th of November, 1808, Murat ordered that the privileges of the Certosa monastery be revoked, its property seized and the monks forced to leave the island. Six months before, on the 15th of May, like an omen comparable to the fall of the ancient lighthouse shortly before Tiberius' death, the high tower which the monks had built in the 16th century for defence against the pirates fell into the sea due to a landslide which blocked the entrance to the Grotta Oscura (pp. 117, 122).

After the fall of Napoleon and the defeat and execution of Murat at the hands of the Austrians, Ferdinand IV returned to Naples and, according to the decision made at the Congress of Vienna, took the name Ferdinand I, ruler of the kingdoms of Naples and Sicily, or what is called *Le Due Sicilie.* With this, one had come full circle, back to the old, familiar Bourbon rule. But Capri could no longer show its famous Grotta Oscura, and its beautiful Certosa was reduced into a prison, later into a hostel for veterans and disabled soldiers, and after 1860 into a military house of correction: all with destruction and disrepair as unavoidable consequences.

Eighteen years later, however, Capri could show an attraction which gradually made the island world famous: Grotta Azzurra, the Blue Grotto.

As pointed out above (pp. 82 f.), this cave was known and visited during the early days of the Roman Empire and later on at least from the 17th century onwards, when it was named Grotta Gradola.

Consequently, the grotto was not discovered, when on the 17th of August, 1826, it was visited by the German poet August Kopisch and his compatriot, the painter Ernst Fries, together with the innkeeper and notary Giuseppe Pagano, the fisherman Angelo Ferraro, and a mule driver named Michele Federico. The two Germans were so impressed by the visit that they immediately proposed to give the cave a more poetical name, Grotta Azzurra. The new name met with favour, and the excursion was soon spoken of as « the discovery of the Blue Grotto ».

In reality, of course, this « discovery » only means that the cave became known to educated people outside the island and its surroundings. Kopisch himself narrates that he and Fries were drawn to the undertaking by Pagano's tales of the adventure of the two priests, of how the cave was said to be inhabited by evil spirits, monsters and sirens, of how fire and smoke were seen pouring out of its entrance which expanded and contracted seven times daily, etc. Thus, Ferraro and other

fishermen before and during his time no doubt knew of the
existence of the cave, although probably very few had ever
entered it because of its bad reputation and difficult access,
even with a moderately rolling sea.

The « discovery » of the Blue Grotto, and the cessation
shortly afterwards of the centuries-old threat from the pirates,
made Capri a more and more attractive goal for travelling
poets, authors, and painters. Fries and Kopisch made the first
pictures of the interior of the cave, followed shortly after by
the Dane Frederik Thöming, who in 1833 made one of the
best and most realistic paintings of the grotto ever done, now
to be seen in the Thorwaldsen Museum in Copenhagen. But
it took some years before the ill-famed cave acquired its new
wide-spread celebrity as a colourful wonder of nature.

Kopisch himself seems to have been very slow to realize
the importance of his « discovery », since for a long time he
was content merely to have written a short account of the
event in the guest book of the Albergo Pagano, retold in Gregorovius' Wanderjahre in Italien, and to describe it in two
letters to his mother which were published much later in the
magazine Der Bär, vol. 20, Berlin 1894, no. 33-36. It is also
significant that Baron August von Platen never mentions the
grotto in his diary, although he met Kopisch in Naples and
spent three weeks on Capri in 1827, where he wrote his
eclogue Die Fischer auf Capri.

The young neoromantic poet Wilhelm Waiblinger, on the
other hand, contributed greatly to the fame of the Grotto
through his imaginative prose narrative entitled Das Märchen
von der Blauen Grotte. He stayed on the island for a month
in the autumn of 1828, and was buried a good year later in
the non-Catholic cemetery in Rome, ravaged by wine, love,
consumption and blood-letting. He gives much interesting information about the island in his letters as well, saying that
it was full of fortifications and semaphores — all unmanned.
In his third letter he mentions the Grotta Azzurra, saying that
« some Germans maintain that they have discovered it », which

136

he tries to disprove by referring to the cave described in Domenico-Antonio Parrino's Di Capri, il Seno Cratere (1700) — without realizing that Parrino is talking about the Grotta Oscura, truely obscure since the landslide in 1808. More learned men than Waiblinger have since been guilty of the same confusion: Schoener, Furchheim, Günther, MacKowen, Dibelius, and Kyrle. The poet, however, makes a more serious mistake in both his Lieder aus Capri and Das Märchen von der Blauen Grotte, speaking of the Emperor Friedrich Barbarossa as the builder of Castello Barbarossa (above, p. 105). In his saga about the Blue Grotto, he populates the cave with fairies and Moorish rulers bathed in a phosphorescent blue colour. But he never contrived to enter it himself, probably because of the autumn storms.

The first after Kopisch to describe the Grotto in basis of his own observations, was probably the composer Felix Mendelssohn-Bartholdy, who in a letter dated May 28, 1831, published in his Reisebriefe aus den Jahren 1830-1832 (Lipsia 1864) talks about his short visit to the island, the exertion needed to go up and down the ancient steps to Anacapri in the heat of the summer, and the blinding blue light of the cave, whose water was still so transparent that fish, polyps, shellfish and corals could be seen deep down towards the bottom.

It was first through two prose narrations, however, today read by very few or none, that the Grotta Azzurra became the magnet which in the course of time has drawn more and more foreigners to Capri. The first was Hans Christan Andersen's novel The Improvisatore, in which the 28-year old author, not yet famous for his Tales, lets the narrator, the young Italian Antonio, meet the same problems and disappointments that he himself had met, and see the same cities and sceneries that he himself had seen during his first voyage in Italy, 1833-1834. Naturally, it is a nigh impossible task for a northener to descibe Italy as seen by the eyes of an Italian. The Italy of The Improvisatore is mainly the bright and co-

lourful country of the romantics, but Andersen has managed
to depict the dark sides as well and allows Antonio now and
then to muse ironically about the enthusiasm of foreign artists
for the picturesque decay. The quick changes of action and
scenery, and the clearly seen and accurately described situations,
make the novel one that can be read even today with pleasure
by people who are really familiar with Italy. When it was
published in 1835, it was an instant success, was translated
into several languages, and established the author on an international level.

In this novel, a sort of Baedeker and roman-à-clef fused
together, Andersen creates a vivid picture of the Grotta Azzurra. He lets Antonio be flung unconscious into the « Witches'
Hole » by angry waves, where he revives and believes that
he is floating through the blue ether on the way to the Kingdom of God, and where he meets Lara, the blind girl he has
seen in Paestum. At the end of the book, Antonio and Lara,
who has regained her sight, visit Capri and its wonderful
Grotto again, this time as man and wife.

The year after Andersen's visit to Capri, during which
he also made two naive drawings of the Villa Jovis and the
view from Pagano's inn, Alexandre Dumas the Elder arrived
on board a *speronara,* a combination cargo and passenger ship.
In a book entitled Le Spéronare, published in 1841, the pro-
lific author gives a description of the island in which he offers
shockingly incorrect information about its geology and history
with a stylistic brilliance which culminates in the description
of the Grotta Azzurra: « Qu'on se figure une immense caverne
toute d'azure, comme si Dieu s'était amusé à faire une tente
avec quelque reste du firmament, une eau si limpide, si transparent, si pure, qu'on semblait flotter sur de l'air épaisi ».
Twenty-five years later, after contributing to Garibaldi's expedition to Sicily with a cargo of weapons, Dumas came to
Naples with him, where he was thanked for his help by being
appointed Curator of Antiquities. At the same time, the erudite
archaeologist Carlo Bonucci, leader of the excavations in Pom-

peii, as a Bourbon supporter fell out of grace with the new rule and retired to Capri, where his knowledge was used by Dumas to acquire material for and to translate the latter's work entitled I Borboni di Napoli (Naples 1863).

Bonucci's laudable activities as an archaeologist — it was he who discovered and published the finest of all ancient mosaics preserved, the one showing Alexander the Great and Darius at the Battle of Issus — came to a tragi-comical end. He presumed correctly that the « bones of the giants » and « the weapons of the heroes » that Augustus once collected on Capri were fossilized remains of enormous animals of the pleistocene period and artefacts from the Stone Age, similar to those he himself had found in Apulia. But in his zeal to find such objects on Capri, he let himself believe a farmer's tale about a cave full of huge bones on Monte San Michele, and before he had personally examined the cave and its contents, he spread the sensational news through articles and letters that he had discovered just the place where Augustus had made his prehistoric finds. Among others, he wrote to the great French archaeologist, the Duc de Luyne, who of course wished to see proof of the discovery. And Bonucci could find no other way out of the dilemma than to send him fossils and stone tools — from Apulia. He died in 1870, at the age of 71, and has a memorial plaque in the church of Santo Stefano. It fell to his young friend Ignazio Cerio to establish that what the farmer thought were « giant bones » in the cave actually are stalagmites and stalactites — hence the name Grotta delle Stalattiti — and in due time to bring to light himself on Capri such « bones of the giants » and « weapons of the heroes » as those mentioned by Suetonius (pp. 8, 13 ff.).

The ever-widening reputation of the Blue Grotto seems to have created the need in Kopisch to be known to posterity as the one who discovered the wonder. Therefore, he made a somewhat fanciful revision of what he had written ten years before in the guestbook of the Albergo Pagano and published this version, entitled Die Entdeckung der Blauen Grotte, in

1838, adorned of course with tales of Tiberius' orgies. In spite of this, six years later Percy Bysshe Shelley's widow, Mary Shelley, after a visit to Capri stated in her Rambles in Germany and Italy (1844) that the cave was discovered by two Englishmen who by chance happened to swim into it; she probably got that piece of erroneous information from a Nouveau Guide du voyageur en Italie, of 1836.

On the island, however, it was firmly maintained that the real discoverer of the Grotto was the fisherman Ferraro, who was said to have visited the cave already in 1822, four years before Kopisch came to the island. In any case, Ferraro was favoured among the men who rowed foreigners to the Grotto, and it was suggested that he should get a monthly pension, since he had contributed to the fame of his country, created extra sources of income for his colleagues and due to his advanced age would most likely not strain the communal economy for long. In any case, he had a care-free old age: Dumas claims to have seen him sleeping in the sun at Marina Grande, confident that he had at his disposal a set percent of the money earned by the traffic to the Grotta Azzurra.

During the same period, Capri and its Blue Grotto drew a number of German and French painters whose pictures of the cliffs, buildings and people of the island were often reproduced in engravings and lithographs. Philipp Hackert, a friend of Goethe, may be named among the Germans, while among the Frenchmen were Corot, who in 1828 painted a view of Monte Solaro, and Gustave Doré, whose illustrations for Dante's Inferno seem to be inspired by the cliffs and crags of Capri.

As the islanders became aware of how the Blue Grotto drew tourists, they began to search for other caves which because of their colours could also be of use for earning money. They discovered that more than one cave on the island, given suitable weather and a favourable position of the sun, showed certain colour reflections and, therefore, they proceeded to change the name of the Grotta del Turco, beneath Monte So-

140

laro, into Grotta Verde, the Green Grotto, to name a near-by cave Grotta Rossa, the Red Grotto, and to call another one on the east coast Grotta Bianca, the White Grotto. In the cliff above the Grotta Bianca, there is another cave, difficult to reach, which because of its colourfulness and its remarkable stalactites and stalagmites was named « the wondrous », Grotta Meravigliosa, by a German, Hans Heinz Ewers, who climbed up to it in 1902.

About 1850, a young German historian named Ferdinand Gregorovius made his first visit to Capri. He was inspired there to write a tragedy entitled Der Tod des Tiberius, which was published in 1851 and is now wholly forgotten. After a longer visit to the island in 1853, he published a description of its history and inhabitants called Capri, eine Einsiedelei, in which he gave a metric translation of the Hypatos inscription (pp. 38f.) with a fanciful note saying that « in a demoniacal hour Tiberius sacrificed his favourite boy to the Sun ». This description was included in the author's well-known Wander-jahre in Italien and was reissued in 1868 in an illustrated folio edition entitled Die Insel Capri. At a more mature age, Gregorovius wrote, with stricter historical critique, his monumental and fundamental Geschichte der Stadt Rom im Mittelalter.

In his book on Capri, Gregorovius also gives much precise and interesting information on how the islanders earned their living about the middle of the 19th century. They sold cattle and cheese, hunted birds in the spring and autumn and of course took much nourishment from the sea the year round. Furthermore, every year about two hundred young men, mostly from Anacapri, sailed off in March to fish for corals, going as far away as the coast of Africa and not returning until October, while the women at home were busy weaving silk and cotton. Among these industrious weavers, Gregorovius names four sisters in particular, called The Four Altars, because foreign artists burnt their incence of flattery to them, or The Four Seasons, because each one was more beautiful than the others, as the seasons are said to be on Capri.

One of these sisters, Luisa, made an unusual career, vividly described by Edwin Cerio. She awoke unquenchable love in Mr. George Norton, an English remittance man who lived on Capri on money sent him by relatives in England for the purpose of avoiding seeing him at home. He was well-known among the foreign bohemians on the island and had created a great scandal at a garden party arranged for the respectable members of the English colony by the paintress Mrs. Sophie Anderson, famous for her pure and bloodless female figures in the style of the pre-Raphaelites. Mr. Norton, uninvited, presented himself there, wearing top hat and monocle, and stark naked otherwise. Love for the beauteous Luisa, however, seems to have had a purifying effect on Mr. Norton, his intentions were found to be honourable, and his remittances sufficiently large, and so the father of the girl, a respectable baker in Anacapri, at last removed his objection to the foreign suitor. Mr. Norton and Luisa were married and settled down in an old house, with a vineyard and olive trees and live-stock. They lived a simple, healthy and happy life and gradually were accepted into respectable society, to such an extent that Mrs. Anderson asked Luisa and her three sisters to pose for an allegorical composition called The Four Seasons, said to have been her best work.

Both of them would probably have ended their days in simple peace and harmony on Capri if one day Mr. Norton had not received a letter from England informing him that due to a sudden death in the family, he had become heir to the title and the estate, Grantley Castle in Yorkshire. With a heavy heart, Luisa, who had become Lady Grantley overnight, had to take lessons in English and history and then leave her island, her family and friends and her daily tasks in kitchen and garden to learn how to be mistress of a large castle with butler, servants, chamber maids and a French cook, and finally to be instructed by a strict aunt of Sir George's how she should curtsey when in due time she was to be presented to

Queen Victoria and how she should answer the questions the Queen might put to her.

She and the aunt were given a private audience with Queen Victoria at Balmoral Castle, and she managed the curtseying rather well. But when the Queen asked her about Capri, she forgot her instructions and began to expound on her homeland, about the lack of water, and the wine and the olive oil, about her married sisters and how many children they had. « And you yourself? », asked the Queen. « I have only one so far, a son. But you have many, haven't you? » The aunt was beside herself and tried to intercede, but the Queen was amused and showed a portrait in miniature: « This is the eldest one, Edward. » « You were lucky, then, too, to have a boy first », said Luisa. And when Victoria showed her a somewhat larger miniature of the deceased Prince Consort, Albert, she blurted out: « How handsome he was! How you must have suffered! » The Queen was touched by the spontaneous understandig that the warm, open Capriote girl had for her inconsolable sorrow. She could not make her a lady-in-waiting but invited her often to Balmoral as a friend, probably without the aunt.

In 1853, the same year that Gregorovius visited Capri for the second time, a German named Joseph Victor Scheffel arrived there, having abandoned a legal profession to go to Italy and become a painter. Instead, in Pagano's inn, he became a poet. In the space of six weeks, his romantic epos Der Trompeter von Säkkingen was created there, becoming what Edwin Cerio called « the song of triumph of German youth », published in hundreds of editions. It drew scores of Germans to Capri to see the place where the poem was conceived, despite the fact that the trumpeter Werner and his beloved Margaretha had nothing to do with Capri. The island is mentioned only in the introduction, where the poet represents himself as an object of wonder for the inn folk, because he walks back and forth on the roof and wastes paper by writing only short lines in the middle of every sheet. There is also, in the introduction, a cat named Hiddigeigei who advises the poet to experience life instead of studying and writing poems. This cat gave its name to a Bierhalle in Capri, the Zum Kater Hiddigeigei, which for more than fifty years was the favourite meeting-place for all the Germans who visited the island or settled there. An old photograph taken in the beginning of the 20th century shows that the place gradually acquired a more international character and even served Afternoon Tea.

Some years after the course of Scheffel's life changed on Capri, the same thing almost happened to a young German zoologist named Ernest Haeckel. He arrived on the island in 1859, planning to continue the studies of the fauna of the Bay there that he had started in Naples. Once on Capri, however, he was so taken by the beauty of the island and the romanticism of the artist's life that in one of his letters to his fiancée, printed in 1921 in a book entitled Italienfahrt, he confided to her that his desire to be a landscape painter would have tempted him to leave biology, had his talent equalled his leaning. Haeckel made many landscape studies on Capri but returned wisely to zoology. Instead of becoming a probably mediocre artist, he gained distinction as one of those who defended and developed Darwin's theories of evolution. His artistic talent stood him in good stead, however, as is seen in his excellent drawings in works such as Radiolaria (1887) and Kunstformen der Natur (1899-1904).

Because the famous Blue Grotto, the beautiful nature and the pretty and picturesque inhabitants of Capri began to attract more and more foreigners around the middle of the 19th century, a new source of income was made available for the Capriotes. This occurred at a time when many of the old and natural sources had begun to fail. The confiscation of the property of the Certosa monastery and the banishing of its monks caused a decline in the agriculture of the island. The wine production dried up completely when the phylloxera destroyed the grape vines of the island in the 1850's, and the sulfur spraying which followed in an attempt to protect the plants from the parasite damaged the quality of the wine. Silk production tapered off and finally ceased completely. The coral fishermen no longer needed to fear the pirates, but their catches dwindled.

The islanders, however, quickly became conscious of the new source of income. Mary Shelley describes the begging on Capri as a great nuisance, and even an Italian, the Neapolitan engineer Francesco Alvino, who visited the island in 1837 and the next year published a little illustrated book entitled Due Giorni a Capri, was struck by their begging. « As soon as a foreigner shows his face », he writes, « all of them, rich and poor, adults and children, gather around him and beg loudly for money ». Sixteen years later, Gregorovius stated that begging had reached its acme on Capri. It was only in the course of time that the Capriotes realized that they could acquire money from the tourists in ways more honourable and more effective.

CAPRI AFTER 1860

During the years immediately preceeding and following
the fall of the Bourbon monarchy and the creation of the Kingdom of Italy, the doomed Church State, governed by the reac-
tionary Pope Pius IX, was linked to an untrustworthy or
hostile outside world, surprisingly enough, by the new revolutionary means of communication: the railroad. The line that
connected Rome with the port of Civitavecchia and improved
connections with Genoa and French ports was inaugurated in
1859. Three years later a line between Rome and Naples went
into service. In 1866, Rome was connected with the North
Italian and Middle European railroad net through the line to
Florence, which in 1864 had become the site of the provisional
government for the new Italy. Travels to Rome, which in 1870
ceased to be the stagnating capital of the Church State and
became the new, rapidly changing capital of Italy, as well as
to the down-graded but always alluring Naples, could now be
undertaken in a safer, more speedy and more comfortable way
than in the days of the postal stage-coaches, the hired vetturini,
the bad inns and the feared bands of bandits. Simultaneously
improvements in the travellers' lodging, in combating vermin,
in street cleaning and in general hygiene gradually became no-
ticeable.

The result of all this was a greatly increased stream of
travellers to Italy from the countries beyond the Alps. The
large majority of them had individual goals, according to their
cultural activities and interests. They were poets, authors, journalists, painters, sculptors, architects, historians, archaeologists,
art historians, biologists, or simply people seeking cultural en-
richment in general. One travelled, now as before, alone or

146

with a good friend, sometimes with one's wife or entire family, without fixed plans, without hurry, and without worrying about not being able to find lodgings.

From about 1860, Capri too got its share of the stream of travellers, due to the establishment of steamboat service between Naples and the islands of the Bay. Voyagers now had a quicker and surer crossing, even if they had to change to rowboats off Marina Grande and often had to be carried ashore from them. Capri had not had a sheltered harbour since the Roman breakwater was left to crumble, and it was not to have a new one until the end of the 1920's. The Swedish water-colour painter Egron Lundgren, who stayed some days on Capri after having spent the month of May, 1872, on Ischia, says in one of his travel books that the steamboat from Naples went first to Sorrento and then directly to the Blue Grotto on Capri, where it dropped anchor while the passengers entered the cave in rowboats. The Grotto was clearly considered at this time to be the first and most impressive thing to see on the island. Lundgren found, however, that « nothing is more magnificent than watching the sun sink into the sea behind Ischia or the moonshine cast its broad shadows in the deep dells under the terrible precipices, where you can still imagine that the pale spectre of Tiberius is wandering about ».

Those whose journeys included Capri belonged primarily to the groups mentioned above, and the majority naturally set aside considerably less time for the little island than for Rome, Florence and Naples. Some, however, stayed for longer periods, occupied with writing and painting. And there were even those who stayed on year after year, sometimes up to their death, because they found that on this island they could live the kind of life they wished, whether they were retired people seeking a calm pleasant old age or people who, for one reason or another, had come into conflict with their relatives, their social class, general opinion or political powers in their home countries.

The Germans came in droves and for a time turned Capri into a Klein-Deutschland. By tradition their favourite haunts were the Albergo Pagano and Zum Kater Hiddigeigei. They drank much beer, carrying on socially and often quite noisily, and were proud of their Kaiser, their Bismarck and the military strength and scientific achievements of their mother country. There were also many Englishmen, but they kept more to themselves. Frenchmen, Scandinavians, Americans and Italians from the mainland were less in number. During the early 20th century, many Russians stayed on the island in voluntary or forced exile from the tyranny of the Tzarist regime.

Many of these visitors were highly talented people who were already or soon to become famous as philosophers, poets, authors, artists, scientists or politicians, such as Friedrich Nietzsche, Paul Heyse, Gerhart Hauptmann, Rainer Maria Rilke, Ellen Key, John Galsworthy, D.H. Lawrence, Joseph Conrad, George Bernard Shaw, Compton Mackenzie, Francis Brett Young, Louis Golding, Emil Ludwig, Franz Werfel, Maxim Gorky, Lenin, the painter Oskar Kokoschka, the historian Theodor Mommsen, the bacteriologist Emil Behring. Some of them completed more or less important works during their stay on Capri. But the island itself rarely figures in these works; among the exceptions may be mentioned the short stories by the Nobelprize winner Heyse and, much later, Ada Negri's Canti dell'Isola. The beautiful island evoked quite varied reactions in many of the authors. In a letter, Ivan Turgenev calls Capri a miracle, an incarnation of beauty. André Gide, on the other hand, writes in his Journal that he found the island unbearable and the colour reflections in the Blue Grotto a disappointment. Rilke, seeking solitude on Capri in the winter and spring of 1906-07, vents his irritation in many letters: the island is flooded with admirers, and there is « too many mountains on too little space ». Lenin warned Gorky of the risk of forgetting Russia among the carefree Capriotes.

Those who stayed on year after year on the island and became more or less integrated into the environment also en-

gaged in research, writing or painting, some in addition to this,
or exclusively, in more or less confused philosophical and religious speculations and preachings, often combined with different excentricities. Seldom has any place the size of Capri
during little more than fifty years been able to boast of so
many singular personages as this island in the years between
the unification of Italy and the First World War. All these
foreigners living on Capri are depicted in the witty and comprehensive books by Edwin Cerio, who knew many of these
characters and rendered a lasting service to his island, both
as its historiographer and as the creator of the cultural institution named, in memory of the founder's father, Centro Caprense di Vita e di Studi Ignazio Cerio.

In the following, only some of those are portrayed whose
names are forever connected with Capri, by what they did to
increase the fame and improve the resources of the island, by
their contributions to the study of its history and the exploration of its monuments, or simply by being long-time resi-
dents, well-known if not always well-behaved, in the little cos-
mopolitan world of Capri.

During the greater part of the second half of the 19th
century, the Englishman Henry Wreford lived on Capri, where
he was esteemed by all and sundry. He had been sent to Italy
by The Times to report on the ideas and movements aiming
at the unification of the Italian states. Thus, he can be considered one of the pioneers of journalism and one of the earliest
special correspondents.

One morning in 1842 he took a sight-seeing trip to Capri
— and stayed there for fifty years, marrying a Capriote girl.
But he did not lapse into a life of leisure. He continued to
report to The Times, Daily News, Athenaeum and other newspapers everything that he saw, heard and experienced of what
was happening on the Apennine Peninsula during the decades
of the Risorgimento, the resurrection of a united Italy. He
wrote articles against the Bourbon regime and its brutal me-
thods of punishing those called « liberals », he reported on

Garibaldi's campaigns in Sicily and Calabria, he saw Victor Emanuel II being sworn in on the constitution in the church of San Francesco di Paola in Naples. He expressed, and rightly so, much scepticism concerning Alexandre Dumas' qualifications for the curatorship of antiquities and as editor of the history of Naples which the French author had succeeded in being commissioned to write, with the help of others. « Dumas », he writes to the Daily News in September, 1860, « whatever may be his genius, does not possess the higher qualities of intellect ».

Wreford continued to write articles for The Times about conditions in Italy, among other things the cholera in Naples in 1884, right up to four days before his death in 1892, at the age of 85. A perusal of all his newspaper articles and private papers, now preserved in the Biblioteca di San Martino in Naples and in the British Museum, should give an interesting picture of an important half century of Italian history as seen through the eyes of an intelligent and observant contemporary viewer. His many services for the island he loved, for the poor and for the schools — in 1861 he was appointed honorary school inspector — are enumerated on a memorial plaque in Capri's town hall at the piazza. His gravestone in the foreigners' cementery at Capri tells only what he himself thought best and most important: FOR FIFTY YEARS A RESIDENT OF CAPRI.

Another one of those who spent the greater part of their lives on Capri was the American painter Charles Caryl Coleman. In his youth he had witnessed Garibaldi and Il Risorgimento. He returned to Italy in 1864, spent some time painting in Venice and Rome, and then settled in Capri, where he bought a house which had been Suor Serafina's inn for strangers next to her convent. Regardless of its original character, he turned this house into a dwelling after his own taste, with twisted window columns, glazed tiles and stepped battlements, all of which can still be seen today. In this house, which he named Villa Narcissus and furnished with sundry antiquities, he devoted himself to painting in a romantic-classicistic style, once popular and now forgotten. With his long beard and flowing hair he was a well-known and picturesque figure on Capri for over fifty years, up to his death in 1928, at the age of 87.

During the last quarter of the 19th century, Capri was the setting for another American's original activities. His name was John Clay MacKowen. He was born in New Orleans and had fought in the Civil War on the Confederate side. He had been promoted to the rank of colonel, but after the North's victory had sold his plantations and turned his back on his mother country. After having acquired a medical degree in Heidelberg, as well as some knowledge in classical disciplines, he settled down on Capri in 1876. His home was a medieval tower in Anacapri which he had rebuilt into a house named Casa Rossa, more strange than pretty, blood-coloured, with stepped battlements, Moorish windows, and a Greek inscription over the door, which still greets the inhabitants of Anacapri, now hardly conversant with their Hellenic ancestors' language, with a hearty « Be welcome, citizen of Apragopolis ». In this house MacKowen gathered a collection of fragmentary sculptures from his excavations in the Roman ruins at Damecuta and Gradola, ancient inscriptions from various places, and curios of varying worth. He also wrote a valuable book about the geology, history and monuments of Capri, which was printed in Naples in 1884. But his irascible and despotic temperament, his extravagant actions and his ardently propagated conviction about negro slavery being necessary for the continuance of civilization, made him disliked by nearly all members of the Anglo-Saxon colony, who referred to him as Colonel Slavedriver.

Edwin Cerio, who in his youth was acquainted with Mac-Kowen, tells how the latter got into a serious dispute with Dr. Axel Munthe about a Roman grave: according to the colonel, it contained the remains of a Roman slave who helped

Augustus plan the imperial villa at Damecuta, according to the
doctor, the remains of Commodus' exiled wife Crispina. The
controversy ended with MacKowen's challenging the doctor to
a duel. The duel was never fought, however, as the antagonists
could never agree on the choice of weapons: MacKowen wanted
to settle the issue with pistols, as was the custom in his own
country, while Dr. Munthe, to the delight of the Anglo-Saxon
colony, declared that the only weapon he could imagine using
was a riding whip.

MacKowen also managed to get into an argument with
the authorities of Anacapri. He had bought some land above
the Blue Grotto, laying claim thereafter to everything under
the surface of his property down to the centre of the earth, including the Grotto. When he threatened to seal off its natural
entrance and began digging a private one from his lot, a court
case was instigated which of course in the well-known Italian
way dragged on *ad infinitum*.

Perhaps this and other conflicts lay behind the fact that
in 1900 MacKowen suddenly left Capri and two years later
boarded a ship in Naples for New Orleans, although he had
always sworn never to return to America as long as the neg-
roes were free and the union with the North remained. Once
back in his home town, he got into a fight in a harbour café
with a man who sided with the Union and emancipation. It
ended with the man answering the colonel's insults by shooting
him dead on the spot.

About 1880, a middle-aged Frenchman came to the island
and settled down in the Villa Certosella by the Via Tragara in
Capri. He soon became generally known for his recluse living,
his shortness and his sharp tongue: the islanders called him
'U Francesiello, the English, The Acid Drop. No one knew
why he settled on Capri and what he had been doing before
he came. He was usually seen strutting about in un impeccable
Parisian complet, which greatly increased his reputation for
being somewhat eccentric. But one day he attracted everyone's
attention by appearing in a suit and a cape made from the

handwoven, rough and uncoloured wool from Amalfi which otherwise was used only by fishermen. No innovation in clothing is so extravagant that it cannot become high fashion. Soon the English and Germans on Capri started appearing in more or less picturesque suits made from the same rustic material. Thus, « the little Frenchman » gave rise to the production of handwoven wool fabrics on Capri which continued right up until a few decades ago, when machine-made products took over.

Not until he died in 1903 was it discovered that he, Camille du Locle, had been the director of the Opéra Comique in Paris, that he had composed libretti for a great number of operas, among others the original text to Verdi's Aida, and had launched several other operas, Carmen among them, which, however, received harsh reviews and did not become popular until afterwards. Perhaps it was disappointment which made him leave Paris and his carrier to hide himself on Capri.

A prominent place among the voluntary exiles on Capri is held by the American Thomas Spencer Jerome. After studying history and law first at the University of Michigan and then Harward University, where he received an M.A. in 1887, he became a successful lawyer in Detroit. He even fought meritoriously in the Spanish-American War. On his doctor's advice, however, he gave up Detroit and his practice and settled first in Sorrento and then, in 1908, on Capri as Consular Agent. Here, despite failing health, he applied himself diligently to a critical review and re-evaluation of the sources for the history of Rome and the Roman Empire, especially for the purpose of defending the infamously defamed Tiberius. In 1911 he published a book entitled Roman Memories in the Landscape Seen from Capri. At the end of the same year he held twelve lectures on The Use of Historical Material at the American Academy in Rome. These lectures plus an article entitled The Tacitean Tiberius: A Study in Historiographic Method, published in Classical Philology in 1912, form the essence of his Aspects of the Study of Roman History, published posthumously in 1923. Historical research, however, has profited more from the fund set apart by him in support of the Jerome Lectures, held by prominent historians and archaeologists at the American Academy in Rome and the University of Michigan. A somewhat doctored narrative of his life is found in Somerset Maugham's Cosmopolitans, where he goes by the name of Mayhew.

In his defence of Tiberius, Jerome went so far as to want to set up en imposing inscription in Latin on the Capitol or the Palatine in Rome in praise of the Emperor, previously unjustly discredited but now exonerated by him, Jerome. When this suggestion was declined, Jerome sought permission from the municipal authorities of Capri to set up the inscription on the campanile at the piazza. Perhaps the authorities found it more advantageous for Capri to have an evil and vice-ridden Tiberius than a kind and prudish one: in any case, in the usual way, they decided to delay coming to a decision by naming a committee to investigate the matter and then let the issue go from one authority to the next. Before the question had finished wandering back and forth along the paths of bureaucracy, the ailing Jerome passed away, in 1914, barely fifty years old. On his grave in the cemetery for foreigners in Capri, there is a large stone slab with a long Latin inscription. But the inscription in Tiberius' honour has never been set up.

The names of two Germans are forever connected with Capri, even though their love for the island resulted in misfortune. The one was the artist Wilhelm Christian Allers, the other the cannon king Friedrich Alfred Krupp.

W.C. Allers, a native of Hamburg, came to Capri in 1891. He was a famous artist in his homeland, especially known for his portraits of Bismarck. He continued to portray him even after he settled into his Villa Tragara, with its Gartenlaube and Kegelbahn and Trinkecke. But above all he became the portraitist of the island, immortalizing in drawings created with superior precision his stout fellow-countrymen and fellow-countrywomen, gathered around their beer steins and coffee cups, as well as various local types: old, bearded fishermen, wrinkled old women spinning, enormous matrons, lovely girls and lads. Many of his drawings and watercolours are reproduced in a folio volume entitled Capri (1892), others in La Bella Napoli (1893). Allers quickly became the central figure in the German colony, whose members gathered for gay parties in his villa, where they were offered Hamburger Hausmannskost: Aalsuppe, Schweinebraten and rote Grütze, washed down with beer or wine as they wished.

One morning, however, the Carabinieri came to the Villa Tragara with an arrest order — only to find it abandoned. Donna Lucia, the hostess at the Zum Kater Hiddigeigei, had whispered a warning to Allers the evening before, resulting in his fleeing during the night in a sailboat towards the coast of Calabria, ultimately to end up on another island in the Pacific Ocean. His property was confiscated. The accusations against him seem to be shrouded in mystery: something was insinuated about revenge for unsuccessful blackmail, and something was whispered about liberties taken with his young male and female models and assistants. He never saw Capri again but did ultimately return to his mother country, dying in Karlsruhe in 1915.

Friedrich Alfred Krupp was the grandson of the founder of the large steel works and armament factories in Essen, and at the turn of the century, the richest man in Germany. But he was also a patron of the arts and a philanthropist, supporting artists and caring for the welfare of his employees. In the beginning of the 20th century, he got the idea of financing ships and equipment to investigate the deep-sea fauna in the Bay of Naples. Along with Ignazio Cerio and specialists from the famous Stazione Zoologica in Naples, he participated in the expeditions with great vim and vigour. The results were spectacular: among the organisms which were trawled up from depths of up to 2.000 meters, there were found nine previously unknown species and about eighty which had never been found in the Mediterranean before. The catches also included a little creature shaped as a willow-leaf, which proved to be a remarkable vagabond, ultimately taking the form of *Anguilla vulgaris,* the eel that all Neapolitans eat on Christmas Eve and call *capitone.*

Krupp developed an especial love for Capri. After the day's exhausting deepsea fishing, he often invited the zoologists and crew to Bacchanalian revels in the Grotta Fra Felice, a cave situated on the south side of the island right under the narrow hair-pin turns in the road Krupp generously had constructed along and up the eastern and southern cliffs of Castiglione.

The good-hearted patron was badly rewarded. He did not understand that he set malicious tongues wagging by giving gay wine parties in a cave on the island of Tiberius. Even worse was the fact that Edoardo Scarfoglio, a Neapolitan journalist of the ruthless type which unfortunately has since multiplied, found conditions favourable for attempting to extract money from the cannon king by threatening otherwise to publish certain rumours about Krupp's perverse orgies. When Krupp's secretary brusquely refused him, he made good his threat in a venomous article entitled *Il Capitone.* The title was chosen with great care, for while *capitone* does mean « eel », it also has a quite obvious obscene connotation. The accusations towards this « exploiter of the working class » were of course seized upon and repeated in the Italian socialist paper Avanti and in the German counterpart Vorwärts. These accusations probably worsened Krupp's heart problems, which led to his death in November, 1902. His adversaries were so vulgar that they insinuated that he committed suicide, taking this as a clear concession of gilt.

In 1900, the German painter Karl Wilhelm Diefenbach landed on Capri. He belonged to the corps of eccentric idealists and wanted to paint his philosophy of life. Home in Bavaria he had been in bad favour because he let his children run about naked and wandered around himself long-haired and dressed in a cowl, preaching his vegetarian gospel: « Ihr sollt nicht töten! » (Thou shalt not kill!). As a result, he had been given the abusive name « Der Kohlrabiapostel » (the turnip apostle) in Munich. He had an argument with the Austrian Art Association, who confiscated some of his works on exhibition and auctioned them off. This prompted him to have an exhaustive account of the conflict printed at his own expense in 1895, with the title: « Ein Beitrag zur Geschichte der zeitgenössischen Kunstpflege » (A contribution to the history of present-day custody of art).

The inhabitants of Capri, being used to strange people, viewed him with more tolerance, as he moved into a house near the terrace of the funicular railway and decorated it with a frieze called *Per aspera ad astra.* In this house he painted his monumental compositions, which he showed to tourists for a fee. They also got to hear his exhortation delivered in the listeners' language: Don't kill! Ne tuez pas! Nicht töten! He died in 1913 at the age of 62, just in time to be spared witnessing the slaughter of the First World War.

The municipality of Capri owns forty-five of his canvases, most of them of colossal size, which are exhibited in two large rooms in the Certosa monastery, together with five of his sculptures. Many of them are fantastic landscapes showing the cliffs of Capri rising in bituminous colours toward a night sky dully illuminated by a hidden moon which often casts its pale light on flying seagulls and small nude human figures. Others are pure allegories, with visions of Christ or the Sphinx. One of them, called « Thou Shalt Not Kill », shows a nude man who has thrust his sword into the throat of a stag and, terrified, recoils at the sight of the accusing countenance of God above the horns of the animal.

Among the many eccentric types on Capri was also another Bavarian named August Weber, who lived there for half a century. The library of the Centro Caprense owns his handwritten autobiography, eight notebooks of his with drawings and rhymes in various languages, and a little illustrated book printed in Munich in 1888, with the title « Fünf Jahre auf Capri: Aus dem Skizzenbuch eines Münchener Malers » (Five Years on Capri: From the Sketchbook of a Munich Painter). Judging from these documents, he must have been a man who did what he felt like doing, often quite contrary to what ordinary people call common sense.

According to his own statement, he was born in Munich in 1846 into a well-to-do family, got a good education and then took lessons in painting. Since his classical motifs from the South did not win him much success at home, his mother sent him to Rome after his father's death. He painted and starved for a year in Rome and then took the train to Naples, in spite of his conservative mistrust of the new means of transportation.

In Naples he saved money by sleeping in a haystack near Fuorigrotta for four weeks until he had enough capital to buy a rowboat with which to cross over to Capri, since he did not dare trust the steamboat. Bavarian as he was, he lacked all experience of the whims of the sea and of the proper use of oars. After struggling for eight days against the swells of the Bay, he landed, exhausted from rowing and seasick, at the point of Posillipo west of Naples. He rested there for two months and then set out again in his rowboat. This time, after only two days, and just barely missing being sunk by a steamboat, he arrived at Bagni di Tiberio, where the customs officers took him and put him into goal on the island under suspicion of his being a run-away prisoner.

Once the authorities realized that he was just a crazy foreigner, he was released and settled down near Marina Piccola, first with the legendary fisherman Spadaro, immortalized by innumerable painters and photographers, and then in an old dilapidated fort. He lived the rest of his life on Capri, where he in his turn became a legendary figure. In the course of time he gave up painting and turned to poetry instead, earning what little he needed by giving lessons in German, English, French, Italian and Latin. He subsisted on turnips, radishes, parsnips, carrots, cucumbers and potatoes, boiled together into a mush in a large pot inscribed with the motto *Mihi et Musis,* « to Me and the Muses ». Nourished and inspired by this feed, he produced rhymed proverbs which he wrote down in notebooks or on his shoes and various house walls. Among the best and truest of his poems is this little south German rhyme:

> Die Muse hat mich nie geküsst,
> weil sie doch eine Jungfrau ist.

Which may perhaps be rendered in English in this way:

> The Muse me never gave a kiss,
> because she a pure virgin is.

His love of the Muse, however, did not prevent him from falling in love with a fisherman's beautiful daughter named Raffaela Desiderio, and after many years of persistent courting he overcame her father's resistance to their marriage. He and Raffaela had a son and two beautiful daughters and set up a Beach Pension near Marina Piccola which became a refuge for many beached existences. Among them was the artist Lucy Flannigan, an American of Irish origin, who had come to Italy with a grant of money from Boston. After having landed in Weber's Pension on Capri, however, she decided to stay there and never return home, a decision strengthened by the fact that Weber admired her paintings to such a degree that she could live gratis there year after year; whereas the other guests were divided into three categories according to their ability to pay and were fed accordingly. Weber, however, wrote out her bills conscientiously and gathered them, unpaid, in a huge file which ran from 1902 to 1928, when he died, 82 years old. He and his Raffaela repose in a family grave in the Catholic cemetery in Capri.

Miss Flannigan stayed on at the Pension after Weber's death and continued punctually to leave her bills unpaid, until she had to go to Rome for an operation which had an unfortunate outcome. Her remains were cremated, which led to difficulties vividly described by Edwin Cerio in a novel entitled Il Caso della Signorina Springfield (1936): since she had been a Catholic but despite this had been cremated, the urn with her ashes could not be buried in the cemetery for Catholics, nor in the one for non-Catholic foreigners.

In 1907, the French Baron Jacques d'Adelswärd-Fersen arrived on the island. As the name implies, he had Swedish blood in his veins: his great grandfather is said to have been *le beau Fersen,* who vainly tried to save his beloved Marie Antoinette from the guillotine, and who himself came to a terrible end, being lynched by the mob in Stockholm. The Baron in his youth had been greeted as a new star among French poets when he published, in 1901, his first collection of poems, entitled Chansons légères. But with his next collections of poems, whose contents may be inferred from the titles — Hymnaire d'Adonis à la façon de M. le Marquis de Sade, Adonis aux yeux claire, and Paganisme — and even more through the orgiastic Black Masses he was said to have organized in Paris, he had thoroughly and deeply shocked the public and made an end to any future he might have had in his homeland. He had seen his intended marriage to a young aristocratic lady cancelled and had been tried and sentenced to several months in prison, upon which he had left France.

One can perhaps guess why Fersen chose to settle on Capri. This island had been the scene of the excesses imputed to the Emperor Tiberius, the refuge for Donatien Alphonse de Sade from a death sentence, and the retreat for Oscar Wilde's « dear boy », Lord Alfred Douglas, after the notorious trial in 1895 which resulted in his famous friend's being sent to prison. But Fersen perhaps did not know that when Oscar Wilde two years later, after having served his sentence, came

160

to Capri and appeared in the dining room of the Hotel Quisisana, all of his compatriotes rose from their tables and threatened to leave the hotel if he was permitted to stay there, upon which Wilde left the island.

Fersen had a luxurious home built for him on the edge of the precipice below the Villa Jovis. In this home, named Villa Lysis, as the near neighbour to Tiberius, he devoted himself to writing his sensual poems, which were printed in expensive and carefully proof-read editions, and to a debauched social life with those of similar inclinations, in which opium, cocaine, hashish and erotic perversities played an important part. Edwin Cerio tells a fantastic tale about how Fersen hit upon the idea of having a drama of his performed at night in the Grotta di Matromania. The handsome youth Hypatos, played by the Baron himself, by the light of torches was to be sacrificed to Mithras by Tiberius, played by a fat old cook — when the Carabinieri interrupted the performance and arrested the actors. Anyhow, the orgies in the Villa Lysis sufficed as motivation for the authorities of the island to intervene — they had had enough of the Allers scandal and the Krupp scandal. Fersen was tried and expelled from Italy in 1909, the same year that his novel entitled Et le Feu s'éteignit sur la Mer was published. After five years, however, he got permission to return, and after some trouble with the French military authorities who, obviously ignorant of his deficient aptitude for soldiering, tried in vain to get him to do military service in France, he could once again devote himself to his poetry, his proof-reading and his old life at the Villa Lysis. He died in 1923, devastated by narcotics at the age of 44, and was buried in the foreigners' cemetery in Capri. Fate willed that he, who could not tolerate a single misprint in his poems, had both his first and last names misspelt on his tombstone, which attests that it was raised over the Baron Jaques Adelswàrd Fersen. His stormy life has been told, more or less romanticized, by Compton Mackenzie in Vestal Fire, and by Roger Peyrefitte in L'exilé de Capri.

Among the many intellectual Russians who, opposed to the Tzar's rule, stayed on Capri in the beginning of the 20th century, Maxim Gorky stood out as the great prophet, inspired and somewhat tyrannized by his lovely companion, the actress Maria Fyodorovna, known by her stage name Andreyeva. The couple lived in a house previously inhabited by the bacteriologist Behring, which now became another Casa Rossa. Here Gorky completed a great number of his novels; here also many prominent Russians gathered, among them Ivan Bunin and Feodor Shalyapin, whose bass voice was often heard echoing from the cliffs of the island.

One evening, so it is said, a known Russian revolutionary was expected to the Casa Rossa. He had served many years in prison and then had been staying in Sweden, Denmark, Germany, and Austria, always watched by the police. That same evening, a Capriote barber and guitar player who often cheered moods at the Villa Behring-Gorky, appeared there in leave from the military service, wearing his grenadier uniform. Andreyeva suddenly thought of a practical joke: so when the guest arrived, he was met, to his horror, by a person in uniform who began very formally to read out an Italian warrant for his arrest — but could not keep from laughing when he started to stumble over the difficult name of the guest: Vladimir Ilyich Ulyanov.

In this way Lenin is said to have made his first appearance among the Russians on Capri. For a while he and Gorky were leaders for the « School for the technique of revolution and the scientific education of the propagandists of Russian socialism » which was founded in the Casa Rossa. But very soon it became clear that the mild idealist Gorky and the cold theoretician Lenin had divergent ideas about the means and goals of the revolution. The school was dissolved and replaced with freer meetings at Marina Piccola, where the interpretations of Marx' gospel were followed by songs in Russian mixed with Neapolitan, German and American melodies contributed by curious islanders and foreign hotel guests. Naturally, the Capriotes had no idea of the plans designed to revolutionize the world which were conceived by this serious Russian, who could suddenly for no comprehensible reason burst out in wild laughter but, like Gorky, could never be tought to speak Italian — he did not even succeed in learning to fish, despite the fact that he had Spadaro himself as his teacher. His stays on the island in 1908 and 1910 were commemorated much later by a portrait medallion fixed to a prismatic marble pillar erected in a playground for children near the Parco Augusteo.

Among the many remarkable foreigners who for one reason or another took refuge on Capri around the turn of the last century, we meet the unusual phenomenon of a man who was able to combine a stormy way of living with extensive research and brilliant writing, in which Capri takes a central place: George Norman Douglas.

Through his aristocratic descent, his inheritance of Celtic and Germanic blood, his upbringing in two different countries, and his early and repeated contacts with the Mediterranean world, Norman Douglas seems to have been almost predestinated to become what he was: anti-puritan, anti-conformist, a bisexual hedonist, a polyglot gentleman scholar equally at home in humanistic disciplines as in scientific ones, a connoisseur of fine wines and exquisite wordings.

He was born in 1868 in Thüringen, Vorarlberg, third son of John Sholto Douglas, 15th Laird of Tilquhillie, who ran spinning mills in Bregenz and was married to the daughter of an Austrian baron and his aristocratic Scottish wife. After suffering for two years in English schools, young Norman threatened to arrange his expulsion. He seems to have had good chances of succeeding, for he was allowed to continue his education at the Gymnasium of Karlsruhe, where he acquired solid knowledge of Latin and Greek and devoted himself diligently to studies in biology, mineralogy and music. In addition to his two mother tongues, English and German, he learned Russian, French and Italian. After studies for a diplomatic career, he was sent to the English legation in St. Petersburg. Once there, he brushed up his Russian and felt quite at home, but after two and a half years he found himself forced to go en disponibilité because of a love affair with a high-ranked Russian lady.

Eight years earlier, at the age of twenty, he had visited Naples and Capri and as a diplomat had spent his vacations in the South. Now, in 1896, he left the diplomatic corps and bought a villa on Posillipo west of Naples. Two years later he married an Irish cousin who joined him on voyages to India, Tunis and Ceylon and between times bore him two sons. In the course of time, however, the marriage became less harmonious, and was finally dissolved in 1904. Without wife and children, without any income and half ruined by his and his ex-wife's extravagant life, he moved to Capri to devote himself to research and writing.

Already from the age of eighteen he had published zoological observations in German and English, and in a paper « On the Darwinian Hypothesis of Sexual Selection » (1895) had treated, among other things, a problem fervently discussed by leading zoologists of the time, namely, the origin of the intense colour of the *Lacerta coerulea,* the blue lizard, which is, or was, to be found only on the two outer Faraglioni at the south coast of Capri.

Now he delved into the published and unpublished sources concerning the history of the island and between the years 1904 and 1915 wrote nine erudite and comprehensive monographs on such diverse subjects as the Blue Grotto and its literature, the forestal conditions of Capri, Fabio Giordano's description of the island, Tiberius, Saracens and corsairs on Capri, and the life of the Venerable Suor Serafina. They were printed in small editions, and were reprinted in 1930 in a book with the modest title Capri: Materials for a Description of the Island.

Some of the « materials » form the basis for a collection of fine essays on the Sorrento Peninsula and Capri which

Douglas published in 1911 under the title Siren Land. It had not the great sale that the author had hoped and greatly needed, probably because its playful erudition was far above the educational level of the reading public. It was not until the 20's that it received its due through new editions. An excellent Italian translation from the 40's, which was not allowed to be printed during the Second World War, was published in 1972 in a fine illustrated edition.

In 1912, Douglas published a book on Tunis, entitled Fountains in the Sand, which also proved to be a disappointment as far as sales were concerned. During the First World War, he contrived to get along a few years in London by working for the English Review, writing as well on a description of what he had seen and experienced during travels in southern Italy. The book, published in 1915 under the title Old Calabria, was well received by some discerning critics, but was no great success among readers in general. This is not surprising, since the author seems to take it for granted that his readers are as erudite as he himself. Today, Old Calabria is ranked as a classic in the abundance of outstanding English travel books.

Disappointed and bitter, Norman Douglas managed to return to Capri where, in the summer and autumn of 1916, he completed the novel South Wind. He returned to London just prior to its being published but was forced to flee to Paris before it came out, accused of « criminal assault ». The novel was published in 1917 and earned enormous fame for its author. During the years between the wars, which he spent mainly in Florence and/or in travels in Mediterranean countries, his prestige continued to rise, through works like Alone (1919), Together (1923), In the Beginning (1927) and Looking Back (1923). He was looked upon as a legendary exile, living happily, freed from the hypocrisy and conventions of his native country.

In 1938 he was forced to leave Florence and moved to the French Riviera. When the war broke out he managed to

get from the Riviera to Lisbon. Not until 1942 was he able
to return to a bombed and blacked-out London, where he
stayed for five years. After that, he went back to Capri, where
he spent his last five years, first in a house lent to him by
Edwin Cerio, then in the Villa Tuoro with his friend Kenneth
Macpherson. He was made an honorary citizen of Capri, as
was Benedetto Croce. He died in 1952 at the age of 83, just
a few months before his Footnote on Capri was published.
His gravestone in the foreigners' cemetery in Capri is inscribed,
in addition to his name and the dates of his birth and death,
with three words from one of Horace's odes (II, 3), where
the poet exhorts us to endure the adversities and enjoy the
pleasures of life with equanimity, since all of us, whether we
complain or exult, are driven towards the same end, the
eternal exile of death: OMNES EODEM COGIMUR.

The novel South Wind is a masterpiece of witty and malicious entertaining. It describes, in short, how an Anglican
bishop, Thomas Heard, on a voyage home from his diocese
in Africa, finds his moral views gravely altered during a stop
over on the island of Nepenthe in the Mediterranean, exposed
to the hot breath of the scirocco and the influence from the
many foreigners and natives he meets there: altered to the
extent that he keeps silent about having seen the rascally Mr.
Muhlen disappear without a trace, pushed down from one of
the horrible precipices of the island. The Bishop meets a colourful crowd of peculiar characters. There is the ascetic and
fanatic parish priest, nicknamed Torquemada, who unlike the
other priests has a reputation for absolute chastity and therefore is unpopular. The popular one is his colleague, the fat
Don Francesco, who fishes for people, mainly women, *ad
maiorem Dei gloriam,* and for the fun of the thing. His latest
catch is the Duchess of San Martino, who is of course no
duchess at all, but the widow of a man who perhaps could
have been a Papal Duke if he had lived longer: so why not
call herself a Duchess? There is Madame Steynlin, a strict
Lutheran usually, but temporarily Orthodox because of a

166

penchant for one of the Russians on the island, all of whom belong to a strange religious sect and at last give the villainous Judge Malipizzo a long-desired opportunity to lock them up for an indeterminate length of time. There is the rich, sybaritic Mr. Keith, possessed of an unlimited eagerness to learn, who presents shocking views on morality, education, religion, the art of living and much more. His opposite is the poor Mr. Eames who, after his one and only, unsuccessful and ridiculous love affair, has strict principles, lives on milk and salad, and is interested in nothing but the annotation of an old Latin tome about the history of Nepenthe. There is the alcoholized Miss Wilberforce, who dresses in black when she isn't walking about naked, explaining the former attire by saying that she is in mourning for Don Francesco's lost chastity and the latter by pointing out thas she is following the example of St. Franciscus: is not that good enough? There is further the aesthete Count Caroveglia who acquires a suitable dowry for his beloved daughter by selling his famous Greek bronze Faun from Locri, dexterously made by the Count himself, to the American millionaire Van Koppen, who often arrives at the island in his yacht, on which unmentionable orgies take place, seen by no one but known by everybody. There is, last but not least, the amoral Mr. Parker, a conceited wretch who gets all his useful ideas from his slanderous lady, takes pains with his British appearance and reputation, gets remittances from relatives who prefer not seeing him at home, and shows off as Financial Commissioner of Nicaragua and as President of the Alpha and Omega Club, where he serves his fake whisky, generally known as Parker's Poison.

The many bizarre personages on this island, its Greek name meaning « The Sorrowless », and many characteristics of its topography, lead every initiated reader to think of Capri, even though Douglas disguised it by placing Nepenthe near Africa and having its rocks made of volcanic stone, with no less than twelve curative springs. When the book was published, it created much bitterness in many of the members of the

Anglo-Saxon colony on Capri, who felt themselves maliciously charicatured. Douglas admitted, much later, that « the social atmosphere of Nepenthe is distilled out of Capri » and that certain figures in the novel were inspired by or given traits taken from people he had met on Capri, although the figures in their entirety are ficticious. « No authentic child of man will fit into a novel, history is the place for such people: history, or oblivion », he says in Looking Back.

Mr. Parker, who is so proud of being an Englishman and holds the Italians in contempt, and his gossip-loving lady, who had « that most priceless of all gifts: she believed her own lies », are said to depict in part Mr. and Mrs. Harold Trower, who lived on Capri from the 1890's to 1940. He was a British Consul and wrote a Guide to Capri (1898) and a description of the geology, history, monuments etc. of the island, pretentiously entitled The Book of Capri (1906 and 1924), the value of which lies principally in the many extensive quotations taken from works by I. Cerio, Th. Spencer Jerome, C. Weichardt and others. The remains of the couple now rest in the foreigners' cemetery in Capri, under a column crowned by a sun dial facing north and, consequently, functionless.

Douglas also told who the prototypes were for Judge Malipizzo, the Duchess of San Martino, Madame Steynlin, and Mr. Muhlen, but this is of no interest today, for those models have not their place in history, but in oblivion.

It is tempting to guess that the millionaire Van Koppen with his yacht and his alleged orgies has borrowed some traits from Alfred Krupp, and that the author put many of his own ideas into the mouths of Mr. Keith and Count Caroveglia. One would also be tempted to see a self-portrait in the personage of poor Mr. Eames, who knows everything about the history of Nepenthe — if he hadn't but one love affair, and didn't exist on milk and salad.

AXEL MUNTHE AND VILLA SAN MICHELE

The Swedish doctor and author Axel Munthe has done more for Capri's reputation internationally and for the welfare of its inhabitants than any other single person since the days of Augustus, Tiberius and Queen Joan. Therefore, it seems appropriate to devote a chapter in this book to his life and work, primarily in so far as they are related to Capri.

Axel Munthe was born in Oskarshamn, Sweden, in 1857. He studied medicine, and in 1876, having problems with his lungs, went to Italy. During a brief visit to Capri, he received such strong impressions there that for the rest of his life he was to be drawn to this island.

He overcame his illness and continued his medical studies in Montpellier, France. In 1880, not even 23 years old, he was awarded an M.D. degree in Paris, and then, newly-wed, spent the best part of the next year on Capri. For the following seven years he worked in Paris as a general practitioner. The greater part of his fees probably went towards helping poor and sick Swedish artists. He returned often to Capri in those years and volunteered his help during the fearful cholera epidemic which scourged Naples in 1884. Almost ninety years later, when in 1973 the terrible disease appeared again in the same city, Italian newspapers mentioned him with gratitude.

From 1885 onwards, Dr. Munthe wrote a series of letters and articles for Swedish newspapers, describing his experiences in Naples during the cholera epidemic, in Paris and Rome, and on Capri. These writings were praised by reviewers and collected in a number of books; some of them also appared in English, in books entitled Letters from a Mourn-

ing City (1887), Vagaries (1898), and Memories and Vagaries (1908). Two of his articles, dealing with menageries and
the dogs on Capri, give evidence of the author's great interest
in animals and the protection of animals.

In 1887 Dr. Munthe discontinued his medical practice
in Paris, divorced his wife the next year, and then spent
two emotionally and economically trying years in Anacapri. In
1890, however, he returned to Rome and opened a new practice in Keats' House at the Piazza di Spagna which drew more and more distinguished and wealthy patients of various na-
tionalities, suffering from real or imaginary illnesses. This enabled him to realize a long-cherished dream: to acquire the
ruined chapel of San Michele and an adjacent vineyard in Anacapri, to be able to settle down there in the future.

We know from a letter written by Dr. Munthe in 1896
to an old friend, the Norwegian diplomat George Sibbern,
that in this year work was under way to convert the chapel
into a dwelling-house, that remains of a room with mosaic
floor and wall paintings, belonging to one of Tiberius' palaces, were excavated in the vineyard, and that « many antiquities and hundreds of Greek and Roman coins » were discovered. Later, however, Dr. Munthe began building a new
and larger house, according to his own romantic ideas. The
building advanced by stages, until the house, named after
the old chapel, presented itself as it is described by one of its
first visitors, Henry James, in The Saint's Alfternoon and
Others (1901).

In the course of time, Dr. Munthe acquired other buildings and land as well on Capri: the mountain slope with the
dilapidated Castello Barbarossa above the Villa San Michele,
the old fortress called Torre Materita and its surrounding park,
the Torre della Guardia and the Torre Damecuta with the
ruins of another imperial villa. In his Villa San Michele he
received as friends and patients both the simple villagers of
Anacapri and prominent men and women of the world. From
1892 on, he was consulted by the Crown Princess Victoria

170

of Sweden, was appointed physician to the King in 1903, and was probably active in the building and furnishing of the Casa Caprile in Anacapri, the villa where Victoria lived as Queen for many of her long years af illness.

In 1907 Dr. Munthe remarried, this time with the young, lovely and wealthy Englishwoman Hilda Pennington-Mellor. They had two sons, Peter and Malcolm. Gradually, though, they spent more and more time apart, she and the boys in England or on the family's farm in Leksand, Sweden, he mainly on Capri.

After a reissue in 1909 of some earlier articles, Dr. Munthe did not publish anything for twenty years, except for an Italian edition of the letters from Naples, called La città dolente (1910), and a book published anonymously in 1917 under the title Red Cross and Iron Cross, by a Doctor in France, a narrative based on his experiences as a volunteer doctor for the English Red Cross during the First World War, and which occasioned great bitterness in Germany because of his savage attack on German militarism. His long literary silence probably had several reasons: depression following his divorce in 1888, a practice which became more and more demanding after 1890, crises in his new marriage, and a progressive eye disease which led to the removal of one of his eyes in 1910 and constant protection from strong sunlight for the other.

His eye problem was most likely a contributory factor in his moving in 1910 from the white Villa San Michele and setting up a new home in the dark Torre Materita which he had restored. In the isolation of this medieval stronghold, he devoted himself to writing the book which was to be an international success: The Story of San Michele.

When the book was published in 1929, by John Murray, London, Dr. Munthe was 72 years old. He lived two decades more, but had to leave Capri during the Second World War and lived until his death in 1949 in the Royal Palace in Stockholm, as the guest of King Gustaf V. His time and thoughts during these years were probably much taken up with negotiations for new editions and new translations of the famous book and, during the years in Stockholm, with various plans of returning to Capri, despite his old age and the post-war difficulties.

During the last few years of his life, his thoughts must also have revolved around the Villa San Michele and its future after his death. He finally decided to implement a suggestion that he had discussed with the then Crown Prince Gustaf Adolf and Professor Axel Boëthius: namely, to will the villa to the Swedish State under the supervision of the Swedish Institute in Rome to serve as a residence for « Swedish students, artists, scholars, journalists or other guests » who could be presumed to share the donor's feelings for Italy and classical culture as well as humanistic research in general. The donation was received according to the terms of the will, and the Villa San Michele since then has become an institution serving both culture and tourism, primarily thanks to the efforts of its first curator, the journalist and poet Josef Oliv.

It is not within the scope of this book to discuss the various judgements passed on Axel Munthe as a person, a doctor, and an author. Judging from available evidence, he was a highly and diversely gifted man, with a complicated character, capable of brusqueness and compassion, egocentricity and selflessness, boastfulness and contempt for ostentation and convention. All this, together with his habit of amusing or irritating people with fantastic tales of his experiences, his treatments and his antiques, earned him good and credulous friends and sceptical and malicious enemies, both during his lifetime and after his death.

Not even the worst of his critics can deny, however, that during his many years on Capri Dr. Munthe generously helped sick and poor people in a way that many old islanders can tell about even today, and that his famous book, and his villa made famous through the book, played and still play an important part in the development which made Capri a first-range tourist site, thus enabling its inhabitants to experience a standard of living not even dreamt of by their indigent ancestors.

The Story of San Michele has been hailed by Anglo-Saxon critics as a fascinating masterpiece and, lately, ridiculed by Swedish ones as mendacious, romantic, sentimental, and old-fashioned. Many readers, perhaps most of them, have unsuspectingly considered it a true autobiography and have continued in this belief, though it has been shown that several of the remarkable stories in which Munthe appears, not always as a hero, can not have been experienced by him personally. Other readers have been delightedly indignant by discovering that Munthe lies. The fact, however, that Munthe, like most other authors, took license to invent, to borrow motifs, to repattern reality, ought not to surprise or irritate anyone, especially since in the preface to the 12th English edition of his book, he expressly points out that it is not to be considered as a doctor's autobiography, and that « some of the scenes in this book are laid on the ill-defined borderland between the real and the unreal ».

Of particular interest here is Munthe's description in the book of the discoveries made when the vineyard was transformed into the garden of the Villa San Michele. He tells us of how the diggers came upon Roman valls in *opus reticulatum,* « with nymphs and bacchantes dancing on the intonaco of Pompeian red »; how mosaic and marble floors came to light, as well as a fluted column which in falling had crushed a big vase of Parian marble; and how the earth gave back thousands and thousands of floor slabs of variegated marble, innumerable fragments of Roman sculpture, several broken and unbroken Greek vases, dozens of Greek and Roman inscriptions, a clay pot full of Roman coins, and a grave containing the skeleton of a man with a Greek coin in his mouth. The marble slabs, according to the author, were used for pavements in the chapel and in the new house, the column was raised to support « the little loggia in the inner courtyard »; and the fragments of sculpture, it is intimated, were used for decoration of the garden and the various parts of the building.

The description is made with the power of suggestion that Munthe possessed both as doctor and as author, and apparently has been taken as gospel truth by many readers. This seems to have caused two quite opposite reactions. There are some who have accused the Swedish doctor, more or less openly, of manipulations like those committed by the treasure-hunters of bygone days, of having destroyed the ruins of the Roman villa and erected on their site a building of bad taste, incongruous with the traditional architecture of Capri. And there are others who have praised the doctor for having created a beautiful museum of all the remarkable pieces of ancient sculpture which were brought to light during the construction of his villa. Whereas some sceptical ones have spoken and written with gusto about the *anticaglie finte,* the « faked antique junk », to be seen in Dr. Munthe's collection.

The accusation, the praise, and the ridicule are, all and sundry, unjustified. The house built by Dr. Munthe is of course a « Fremdkörper » on Capri. But it is not an architectural monster like MacKowen's Casa Rossa, of which the critics have no bad word to say. And in the matter of the discoveries made, or said to have been made, during the diggings for the lay out of the Villa San Michele, we are enabled to judge in basis of clear evidence.

The reports of Feola and Mangoni (above, p. 72) about how the ruins of the imperial villa on Capodimonte were brought to light around 1830, only to be destroyed little by little by the land owners, is confirmed by W.J.A. Stamer, who in his book entitled Dolce Napoli (London 1878), speaking of this villa, states that « whatever may be left of the ancient fabric has long disappeared from sight ». Two decades later, when Dr. Munthe began the digging for his villa, it is hardly conceivable that anything more was left of the Roman villa than the remains of the small room and the loggia which, carefully protected by the excavator, are still to be seen in his garden. Without his intervening, these remains, too, would no doubt have been destroyed long ago.

The fact, on the other hand, that the brief reference in the letter of 1896 to the antiquites and coins found in the vineyard is in contrast with the vivid description presented in the book of the manifold discoveries made in the same place, makes us inclined to regard this description as an embellishment of what had occurred some twenty years earlier. And there is evidence for this being so.

There is no reason to doubt that some fragments of ancient sculpture and a lot of marble floor slabs may have been brought to light. But since the Roman villa had been exposed to looting for hundreds of years and its ground to farmers' hoes for almost seventy, the floor slabs can hardly have numbered in « thousands » and the fragments of sculpture can harldy have been « innumerable ». The only fragments specified are « a mutilated head of Augustus split in two » (Fig. 12), now in the possession of Dr. Munthe's heirs, « two bronze hoofs of an equestrian statue », and the leg of a statue, called by the foreman superintending the diggers, « la gamba di Timberio ». And the great majority of the ancient sculptures now to be seen in the Villa San Michele consists of funeral monuments of various dates. They can therefore not have been found on the site of the imperial villa, and many of them originate, demonstrably or probably, from Rome or other places in Latium and Etruria.

As regards the « dozens of Greek and Roman inscriptions » said to have been discovered in the vineyard, the simple truth is that of the 97 inscriptions, all Latin, which now adorn various walls in the Villa San Michele, about two thirds are epitaphs of imperial date. They can with as little likelihood as the funeral sculptures originate from the Roman villa, and at least 23 of them are proved to have been found in Rome, in Velletri or in other places in Latium.

The assertion that « several broken and unbroken Greek vases » were found in the famous vineyard is apt to increase our disbelief in the narration, and in Dr. Munthe's qualifications in archaeology. For such clay vases, imported to and imitated in Italy, for obvious reasons are to be found, undamaged or restorable, only in tombs or other subterranean rooms. Graves with Greek and Italo-Greek vases have been discovered on Capri (above, p. 33). But the chance of finding whole vases of this kind in the earth of fields or vineyards ploughed or hoed for generations is non-existent.

The discovery of « hundreds of Greek and Roman coins » mentioned in the letter is probably no pure invention, though the amount seems to be exaggerated and the coins considered to be Greek may have been of Byzantine origin. But it is interesting to note that in the Story of San Michele the diggers find a whole pot full of Roman coins — a discovery which resembles the one made in 1923 (above, p. 35) when some workers found a vase full of Republican denarii near the Torre della Guardia, which was owned at that time by Dr. Munthe.

The grave with the skeleton of a man, on the other hand, is still to be seen in the garden of the Villa San Michele, above the remains of a wall which probably belonged to a loggia in the imperial villa. It is a poor man's grave, consisting of two rows of roof tiles placed so as to form a ridge over the body. Similar graves have been excavated at Le Parate (above, p. 86). It can hardly have been made until the Roman villa had reached an advanced stage of decay. The coin which the dead man is said to have had in his mouth, if it really existed, can hardly have been Greek, possibly Byzantine.

In addition to the information about the antiquities said to have been discovered in the vineyard, Dr. Munthe also tells us in his book of the provenance ot three other items in his collection.

The sculptured Roman well-head, placed in the small inner courtyard, is said to come from the Convento delle Sepolte Vive, the convent of the nuns « buried alive », in Naples, where the doctor had been working during the cholera epidemic in 1884.

The large marble mask of Medusa, set up in the study, is said to have been found « at the bottom of the sea ». Oral tradition adds that Dr. Munthe, looking with his binoculars from the pergola of the Villa San Michele, some 1000 feet (325 meters) above the surface of the Bay, saw the mask as a cameo through the waters off the Bagni di Tiberio and had divers raise it from a depth of c. 90 feet (30 meters). This is clearly absurd, considering the distance and the ruined state of the mask, whose nose, lips and chin are broken off and restored in plaster. The mask probably was found near the temple of Venus and Roma in Rome, together with tree identical Medusa masks, better preserved, which are now in the Braccio Nuovo of the Vatican Museums.

The Egyptian sphinx of red granite, placed on the parapet of the chapel of San Michele, is said to have been found among the ruins of a Roman villa in Calabria, after Dr. Munthe had seen it lying there in a dream. It is af course impossible to determine what truth, if any, is hidden behind this tale — the riddle of this sphinx must remain unsolved.

There are also in the Villa San Michele a small mutilated statue of Hercules in marble and a marble head perhaps of Apollo which were said to have been found in the garden of the villa as late as 1954 and 1961. This information seems to have been based on misunderstanding or wishful thinking: the sculptures are far too coarsely made to have been suitable for an imperial villa.

Like so many other collectors, Dr. Munthe was reticent about the real provenance of his treasures, and being the imaginative person he was, enjoyed concocting strange tales about how he found them. It surely must have amused him when he saw that these tales were being taken seriously. But obviously he found it futile to try to fool the archaeologist Amedeo Maiuri, who says that in 1939, Dr. Munthe told him straight out that he had bought the great majority of his sculptures and columns from antique dealers in Rome and Naples.

Axel Munthe's collection of antiquities is today the largest of its kind on Capri, although when moving to the Torre Ma-

terita he took some of the best pieces with him (which is
why they are now in the possession of his heirs). The collection, however, is not representative of the ancient art of the
island, nor does it contain any works of extraordinary artistic
value, as certain non-expert flatterers pretend. But apart from
two or three sculptures of doubtful antiquity, it does not
consist either of nothing but forgeries, as other non-expert
denigrators claim. Dr. Munthe was no connaisseur of Greek
and Roman art and obviously did not aspire to form a collection of great archaeological, artistic or historic value, even
if he gladly used superlatives when talking of his « priceless
marbles ». He acquired such works as he thought suitable to
decorate his villa and to dream and fantasize about, which
probably accounts for the many sculptures and inscriptions
commemorating unknown dead and forgotten graves. His written works clearly show the place that death and its problems
had for him.

Thus, the collection should be neither over-estimated nor
under-estimated. In addition to the Egyptian sphinx, made
probably after the New Kingdom (i.e. after about 1000 B.C.),
it contains some interesting works originating from ancient
Italy. There is a votive head of terracotta, which through its
beautiful features, showing influence from Greek art of Phidias'
time, differs from the vast majority of similar mass-produced
temple gifts and allows it to be dated to about 400 B.C. There
is a marble head, unfortunately much worn, which belonged
to a Roman copy of a Greek statue from about the same time,
possibly representing Odysseus. Two Etruscan cinerary urns
and many fragments of Roman sarcophagi are interesting because of the mythological motifs in relief which decorate them.
The funarary relief showing the bust of an old man, with his
name Lucius Careius inscribed underneath, is a remarkable
exemple of the realistic portraiture en vogue during the last
decades of the last century of the Roman Republic. The relief
of a young mother with her child is a good example of another
type of Roman gravestone from about 45-30 B.C. The large

178

Medusa mask is a decorative work, interesting because it probably adorned the temple of Venus and Roma in Rome.

The most important work in the collection is the well-preserved head in marble, traditionally considered to represent Tiberius (Fig. 14). It cannot reasonably have been found where the Villa San Michele now stands, as has been claimed occasionally; if that had been the case, it would certainly have been mentioned in the Story of San Michele. But it is at home on Capri since some seventy-five years ago. It corresponds closely with another portrait head from Centuripe, also considered to represent Tiberius. Both these heads, however, as well as some similar ones, have been identified, more plausibly, as portraits of the Emperor's nephew, Germanicus.

The story about the many remarkable antiquities which were discovered while digging for the garden of the Villa San Michele contains much which is provably true, and much which is probably or demonstrably invented. It ought to be read, not as if it were a report of an archaeological excavation, but as a piece of archaeological poetry, perhaps inspired by what Hadrawa, Feola, Mangoni and other earlier authors tell about columns and marble floors of imperial villas, and of graves containing Greek vases or skeletons with coins in their mouths. Like so much else in this subtle book, the story obviously belongs to those scenes which are set « in the ill-defined borderland between the real and the unreal ».

Possibly, it is just that mixture of Dichtung und Wahrheit, these embroiderings on the canvas of reality, which make this book so captivating for those who love the fanciful, and so loathsome for those respectable ones who cannot tolerate lies. But often, the fanciful embroiderings are more faithful to reality than the naked canvas. It is quite possible that the 18-year old Axel Munthe during his first visit to Capri was never enchanted by a black-eyed Gioia, never met old Maria Portalettere on the « Phoenician Steps », never saw old Mastro Vincenzo dig up *roba di Timberio* from his vineyard — it is possible, or rather, very probable, that these and other scenes described in the famous book are fantasies derived from the half-blind old man's store of later sights and experiences. But none among all those who have written about Capri have managed to give such a fascinating and, in a deeper sense, true and correct picture of life on the island in bygone days, and as it still was some fifty years ago, as Axel Munthe, in the unforgetable introductory chapter of The Story of San Michele.

CAPRI IN THE TOURIST AGE

During the Second World War, Capri was spared from the fate that had befallen is so often in the past, that of being fought for by two enemies, obviously because in the age of the airplane its previous military importance had become obsolete. But the islanders in many ways felt what was happening both near-by and far away. Signora Asta Mazzarella, who came from Denmark to Capri over fifty years ago and still lives in Anacapri, widow of the learned and versatile Antonino Mazzarella (pp. 11, 82), has many things to tell about conditions on the island during the war: about prominent authors, Alberto Moravia, Mario Soldati and others, who took refuge in her pension and were supported by the good meals she could serve them, despite the general lack of provisions; about the wretched Italian soldiers who, badly clothed, badly shod, without ammunition and sanitary essentials, were supposed to defend the island while the Allies' bombers thundered overhead on their way to drop their devastating loads over Naples; and how everything changed once the Anglo-American forces had conquered Salerno and Naples, and American officers and soldiers had lovely Capri for rest and recreation. In his book entitled Sweet is War (1954), Malcolm Munthe, son of Axel Munthe, tells how the anti-fascist philosopher and historian Benedetto Croce with his wife and daughter was saved at the very last minute from the Germans, who still held Sorrento, and was brought over to Capri.

Since the end of the war, Capri has naturally had a share of the rapid economic, technical and social development which has taken place in the industrialized countries of the world, once the consequences of the destruction had been eliminated. Most noticable on Capri of the post-war phenomena are the groups of tourists arriving on chartered planes with their guides. This well-organized mass tourism has obvious advantages. It allows even those who lack knowledge of foreign languages and have limited economic resources to leave an often dreary and hectic job and get some idea about other countries, their sceneries, inhabitants and art treasures in an inexpensive and easy way. And the tourist countries receive a large and often well-needed addition of foreign currency.

But like everything else in human life, this too has its disadvantages. The programs for the group travels by necessity become stereotyped, limited to certain famous places, monuments and museums, sometimes merely to hotels, restaurants and beaches. The guides have far too often inadequate knowledge of their subjects, and the travellers all too often hear things that, in the best of cases, go in one ear and out the other. Even worse, the mass invasion of tourists often results in destruction of what they come to see, through wear and tear, souvenir hunting which stimulates clandestine excavators and art thieves, and worst of all, by attracting ruthless constructors who short-sightedly and without opposition from sleeping, duped or bribed authorities erect banal or hideous multi-storey buildings in the most beautiful areas of the countryside and the most glorious historical quarters of the cities. And, in addition to all this, mass tourism often causes a decline of taste and moral in the host countries, where people easily fall prey to the temptation of padding the bills and selling cheap and common souvenirs at high prices to inexperienced and trusting foreigners.

Some of these disadvantages have left their mark even on Capri, but in general, the island has received most of the good things and avoided the worst of the bad ones connected with this sort of tourism, and with the post-war development in general. Between the months of May and October, the island is inundated with foreigners from different countries, who often dress or undress themselves in many bizarre ways. Led by their guides, the tourists in general get to visit two easily accessible attractions, the Grotta Azzurra, which has retained its old fame, and Axel Munthe's San Michele, which has become the new highlight in the pre-arranged programs. Few of the visitors care to see the Certosa monastery, even fewer summon up the energy — since donkeys are no longer available — to walk the upward path to the Villa Jovis, and many leave the island sure in the belief that they have seen all there is worth seeing after visiting the Blue Grotto, the Villa San Michele and one or two night clubs.

But this mass tourism has converted the long-standing poverty of the island to a prosperity never dreamed of before. Money has been earned enabling people to modernize old buildings and build many new hotels, pensions, restaurants and cafés. Shops with all kinds of enticing wares, not just tourist junk, line the main streets of Capri and the road to the Villa San Michele. Wealthy men from Naples and Milan have erected expensive villas on the island, which are closed up six months or more of the year. The asphalt-coated road between the towns of Capri and Anacapri which replaced the « Phoenician Steps » a hundred years ago has been extended all the way to the Grotta Azzurra and to the lighthouse at Punta Carena. The harbour has been widened by building a second breakwater. Fast *aliscafi,* « wing boats », shuttle between Naples and Capri. A plant for desaliation of sea water has been constructed between Capri and Marina Grande which in the future will perhaps eliminate the need to transport fresh water from the mainland in tankers.

But before it is drinkable, the water of the Bay has to be cleansed of much more than just salt. It is incredibly polluted by the sewage from Naples and the many towns all around the Bay. The water in the Blue Grotto is no longer as transparent as it was in bygone days, and the delicious mussels sometimes cause hepatitis and also received the blame for the cholera epidemic which broke out in Naples in 1973.

Many things which formed the charm of Capri in the olden time have changed or disappeared. The old Zum Kater Hiddigeigei, so rich in tradition, is no more: it was changed into a modern restaurant, then lately into a radio and TV shop, and now the squawk of new-fashioned katzenjammer music resounds under the arched ceiling which reverberated from laughter and gay songs in the past. The virgin greenery of the island has become more and more dotted with white villas. Those who sing the praises of the good old days may find this irritating and justly criticize many of the new builindigs — as far back as the 20's, Edwin Cerio called iron girders and concrete the arch enemies of the traditional architecture of the issland. But anyhow, we ought to be thankful for the fact that new buildings on Capri are usually more or less in keeping with tradition, and that at least we do not have to see here those kinds of multi-storey houses and tasteless noveau riche villas that destroy cities and countryside in many parts of Italy, and everywhere else.

Capri, however. has not become only a centre for an often superficial and frivolous tourism, it has also acquired a number of cultural institutions. The most important of them is the Centro Caprense di Vita e di Studio Ignazio Cerio, founded by Edwin Cerio, which since 1949 is a foundation for the furthering of historical, archaeological, geological, biological and oceanographical research concerning Capri and its surroundings. Its library, museum, concert hall and conference rooms are housed in the Palazzo Cerio, mentioned above (pp. 9, 98). Next comes Axel Munthe's Villa San Michele, which since 1950 is not only a tourist attraction and a guest house for Swedish scholars, artists and authors, but also carries on cultural activities through art exhibitions and concerts in the chapel of San Michele. The Swedish station for bird studies, located in the Castello Barbarossa, is closely connected to the Villa San Michele and active in the spirit of Dr. Munthe's interest for the life of animals. Finally, it is to be mentioned that Italian authorities have appointed a committee instructed to plan for a thorough restoration of the Certosa monastery and the institution of a museum there intended to house the works of ancient sculpture from Capri owned by the Italian State, Diefenbach's paintings and sculptural works, and other objects illustrating the history of the island. A history well worth to be studied and remembered.

BIBLIOGRAPHY

Literature about Capri, its geological formation, its prehistory and history, its ancient monuments, its architecture and art, its flora and fauna, etc. is very extensive. Furchheim's bibliography (see below) in its enlarged edition of 1916 includes no less than 655 works concerning Capri. Since it was published, a large amount of books and essays on relevant subjects have come out. Here, however, are given only those works which offer important information and research results concerning the island's creation and human activity on and around it. The ancient sources are included in the text.

LITERATURE WITH GENERAL AND MIXED CONTENTS

Fabius Jordanus (Giordano): Historia Napolitana. Manuscript XIII-B 26 in the Biblioteca Nazionale in Naples. The section De Capreis Insula is published by Norman Douglas (see below) .

Julius Caesar Capacius (Capaccio): Urbis Neapolis a secretis et civis historiae neapolitanae libri duo, etc. Neapoli 1607.

Domenico Romanelli: Isola di Capri. Manoscritti inediti del Conte della Torre Rezzonico, del Professore Breislak, e del Generale Pommereul pubblicati dall'Abate Romanelli con sue note. Napoli 1816. Contains: 1) Descrizione dell'Isola di Capri fatta dal Conte Castone della Torre Rezzonico nel 1794; 2) Note dell'editore; 3) Mineralogia dell'Isola di Capri. Lettera del sig. Breislak; 4) Dimensioni geografiche di Capri. Lettera del Generale Pommereul al sig. Hadrava.

Rosario Mangoni: Ricerche storiche sull'Isola di Capri colle notizie più rilevanti sulla vicina regione del Cratere. Napoli 1834.

Ferdinand Gregorovius: Capri, eine Einsiedelei, in Wanderjahre in Italien, Band 1, Leipzig 1856; new edition: Die Insel Capri, mit Bildern und Skizzen von K. Lindemann-Frommel in Folio. Leipzig 1868. Die Insel Capri, Idylle vom Mittelmeer. Leipzig 1880.

John Clay MacKowen: Capri. Naples 1884.

Antonio Canale: Storia dell'Isola di Capri dalla età remotissima sino ai tempi presenti. Napoli 1887.

Paul Oppenheim: Die Insel der Sirenen von ihrer Entstehung bis zur Gegenwart. Eine populäre Darstellung der physischen und politischen Geschichte der Insel Capri. Berlin (1890).

Reinhold Schoener: Capri. Natur, Volkstum, Geschichte und Alterthümer der Insel. Wien, Pest, Leipzig (1892).

Manfredi Fasulo: L'Isola di Capri.Istoria — Usi e costumi — Antichità — Bibliografia. Seconda edizione, Sorrento 1906.

Harold E. Trower: The Book of Capri. Naples 1906. Second edition, Naples 1924.

Norman Douglas: Siren Land. London 1911. Revised edition 1923. In New Adelphy Library 1927 and 1929. As Penguin Book no. 625, 1948. Illustrated Italian edition in Biblioteca delle Due Sicilie, Testi e Documenti sul Mezzogiorno, I, with the title La Terra delle Sirene, traduzione, introduzione e nota bibliografica di Giuseppe Viggiani, a cura di Domenico Viggiani. Edizioni Scientifiche Italiane, 1972.

Friedrich Furchheim: Bibliographie der Insel Capri und der Sorrentiner Halbinsel sowie von Amalfi, Salerno und Paestum. Leipzig 1916.

Norman Douglas: Capri, Materials for a Description of the Island. Florence 1930. Contains nine essays which were originally published separately, signed N.D. in London and Naples between the years 1904 and 1915, with the following titles: The Blue Grotto and its Literature. London 1904. — The Forestal Conditions of Capri. Napoli 1904. — Fabio Giordano's

Relation of Capri. Napoli 1906. — The lost Literature of Capri. Napoli 1906. — Tiberius. Napoli 1906. — Saracens and Corsairs in Capri. Napoli 1906. — The Life of the Venerable Suor Serafina di Dio. London 1907. — Some Antiquarian Notes. Napoli 1907. — Disiecta Membra. London 1915. — With Index. London 1915.

Enzo Petraccone: L'Isola di Capri. Con 140 illustrazioni. Seconda edizione aggiornata da Manfredi Fasulo. In the series « Italia Aristica », Bergamo 1913.

Immanuel Friedländer: Capri. Tradotto da Angelo de Angelis. Roma 1937.

Amedeo Maiuri: Breviario di Capri. Napoli 1937. Seconda edizione, Padova 1947. German ed.: Capri, Mythos und Wirklichkeit. Napoli 1938.

Edwin Cerio: L'Ora di Capri, Capri 1950. German ed.: Capri, ein kleines Welttheater im Mittelmeer. München 1954. English ed.: The Masque of Capri. London 1957.

Norman Douglas: Footnote on Capri. With 48 photographs by Islay Lyons. London 1952.

Amedeo Maiuri: Capri, Storia e Monumenti. Itinerari dei Musei, Gallerie e Monumenti d'Italia, no. 93. Roma 1957. French ed.: Capri, Historie et Monuments. Roma 1956. English ed.: Capri, its History and Monuments. Roma 1958. German ed.: Capri, Geschichte und Denkmäler. Roma 1969.

Alma Siracusa - Ermanno Vuotto: Capri porto dei sogni. Napoli 1957.

Arvid Andrén, Edwin Cerio, Amedeo Maiuri i. a.: Boken om Axel Munthe, Capri och San Michele. Malmö 1957. Contents: Axel Munthe, Den skönsta pärlan i Napolis krona. — Amedeo Maiuri, Capri under förhistorisk tid och under antiken. — Edwin Cerio, Röster från Capri. — Alma Siracusa, Capri av i dag. — Josef Oliv, Axel Munthes liv och verk. — Malcolm Munthe, Min far Axel Munthe. — Bror Olsson, Axel Munthe som författare. — Dens., Bibliografi över Axel Munthes skrifter. — Arvid Andrén, Axel Munthes San Michele. — Dens., Den antika konsten i San Michele. — Hilding Thylander,

Latinska inskrifter på San Michele. English ed.: The Story of Axel Munthe, Capri and San Michele. Malmö 1959.

Humbert Kesel: Capri. Biographie einer Insel. München 1971.

Luciano D'Alessandro: Così Capri. 116 photographic reproductions partly from Centro Caprense's photo archives, with preface by Graham Greene and a short bibliography by Noemio Borbone. Milano 1972.

CAPRI'S GEOLOGICAL FORMATION AND ATTRACTIONS

Giuseppe Ruffo: Sulla Grotta Azzurra di Capri. Memoria del Marchese Giuseppe Ruffo, Socio ordinario della R. Accademia delle Scienze. Napoli 1836.

Macedonio Melloni: Alcune ricerche accompagnate da esperimenti sulla cagione della luce azzurra che illumina la grotta di Capri, in Rendiconto delle adunanze e de' lavori della R. Accademia delle Scienze, Anno V, Napoli 1846.

Johannes Walther: I vulcani sottomarini del golfo di Napoli, in Bollettino del R. Comitato Geologico d'Italia, 22. Roma 1886.

Paul Oppenheim: Die Geologie der Insel Capri. Berlin 1891.

Hermann Karsten: Zur Geologie der Insel Capri, in Neue Jahrbücher für Mineralogie, Geologie etc., 1, 1895, 2, 1898.

Robert T. Günther: Contributions to the Study of Earth Movements in the Bay of Naples, in Geographical Journal, 22, London 1903.

Friedrich Furchheim: Die Blaue Grotte auf Capri, in Deutsche Rundschau für geographische Statistik, 29, 1907.

Giuseppe De Lorenzo: L'Isola di Capri, in Rendiconti della R. Accademia dei Lincei, Classe di scienze fisiche, matematiche e naturali, 16, 1907.

Gaetano Rovereto: L'Isola di Capri. Genova 1907.

Raffaello Bellini: Studio sintetico sulla geologia dell'Isola di Capri, in Atti della Società Italiana di Scienze Naturali, 55, Pavia 1916.

G. Gianfranceschi: I fenomeni luminosi della Grotta Azzurra. Capri 1930.

Giorgio Kyrle: Le grotte dell'Isola di Capri. Studio del carsismo dell'isola con riguardo ai movimenti di spiaggia. Istituto Geografico Militare (Firenze) 1947.

PREHISTORIC CAPRI

Salomon Reinach: Le musée de l'Empereur Auguste, in Revue d'Anthropologie, ser. 3, tome IV, 1889.

E. Regalia: Sul museo dell'imperatore Augusto, in Archivio per l'Antropologia e la Etnologia, 19, 1889.

Carlo Bonucci: Monumenti antistorici scoverti dal 1863 al 66 nelle provincie napolitane per Carlo Bonucci al Signor Duca di Luynes. Napoli 1866.

Abele De Blasio: Gli avanzi preistorici della Grotta delle Felci nell'Isola di Capri, in Bullettino di Paletnologia Italiana, 21, 1895.

Luigi Pigorini: Materiali paletnologici dell'Isola di Capri, in Bullettino di Paletnologia Italiana, 32, 1906.

A. Portis: È dimostrata la contemporaneità dell'uomo paleolitico con l'Elephas antiquus ecc.?, in Bullettino della Società Geologica Italiana, 31, 1907.

V. Giuffrida Ruggieri: Nuovo materiale paleolitico dell'Isola di Capri a facies eolitica, in Atti della Società Romana di Antropologia, 14, 1908.

Gaetano Rovereto: Studi di geomorfologia, I. Genova 1908.

Rafaello Bellini: L'uomo preistorico nell'Isola di Capri, in Rivista mensile di scienze naturali « Natura », 1, Pavia 1910.

F. Bassani - A. Galdieri: Scavo geologico eseguito a Capri, in Atti della Società Italiana per il Progresso delle Scienze, IV Riunione, Napoli, ottobre 1910. Roma 1911.

F. Bassani - A. Galdieri: Strumenti « chelléens » dell'Isola di Capri, in Bullettino di Paletnologia Italiana, 37, 1911.

Ugo Rellini: La Grotta delle Felci a Capri, in Monumenti Antichi pubblicati per cura della R. Accademia Nazionale dei Lincei, 29, 1923.

Friedrich von Duhn: Capri, in Reallexikon der Vorgeschichte, II, Berlin 1925.

G. De Lorenzo - G. D'Erasmo: L'uomo paleolitico e l'Elephas antiquus nell'Italia meridionale, in Atti della R. Accademia delle Scienze fisiche e matematiche di Napoli, Vol. 19, serie 2ª, N. 5, Napoli 1932.

Giorgio Buchner: La stratigrafia dei livelli a ceramica ed i ciottoli con dipinti schematici antropomorfi della Grotta delle Felci, in Giornale di Paletnologia Italiana, 64, 1954-55.

GREEK AND ROMAN CAPRI

Giuseppe Maria Secondo: Relazione storica dell'antichità, rovine, e residui di Capri, umiliata al Re da Giuseppe Maria Secondo, Governatore dell'Isola. Napoli 1750. New ed., Napoli 1808.

Norbert Hadrawa: Ragguagli di varii scavi, e scoverte di antichità fatte nell'Isola di Capri dal Sig. Hadrava, e dal medesimo comunicati per lettere ad un suo amico in Vienna. Napoli 1793.

Norbert Hadrawa: Norbert Hadrawa's freundschaftliche Briefe über verchiedene auf der Insel Capri entdeckte und ausgegrabene Alterthümer. Aus dem Italiänischen übersetzt. Mit Kupfern. Dresden 1794.

Giuseppe Feola: Rapporto sullo stato attuale dei ruderi Augusto-Tiberiani nell'Isola di Capri. Manoscritto inedito del 1830, pubblicato ed annotato dal nipote Dott. Ignazio Cerio di Capri. Napoli 1894.

Rosario Mangoni: Ricerche topografiche ed archeologiche sull'Isola di Capri da servire di guida a' viaggiatori. Napoli 1834.

F. Alvino - B. Quaranta: Le antiche ruine di Capri disegnate e restaurate dall'architetto Francesco Alvino, ed illustrate dal Cavalier Bernardo Quaranta. Napoli 1835.

Julius Beloch: Campanien. Geschichte und Topographie des antiken Neapels und Umgebung. Berlin 1879. 2. Auflage, Breslau 1890.

Corpus Inscriptionum Latinarum : Vol. V: 2 (Berlin 1882), nos. 8409, 8958; Vol. X: 1 (Berlin 1883), nos. 6806-6810; Ephemeris Epigraphica, VIII, 1899, Additamenta ad Vol. X, nos. 670-673/4.

Michele Ruggiero: Degli scavi di antichità nelle province di Terraferma dell'antico Regno di Napoli dal 1743 al 1876. Documenti raccolti e pubblicati da Michele Ruggiero. Napoli 1888.

Inscriptiones Graecae: Vol. XIV, Inscriptiones Graecae Italiae et Siciliae, edidit G. Kaibel (Berlin 1890), nos. 67, 896-902, 897a, 898a, 901a.

Carl Weichardt: Das Schloss des Tiberius und andere Römerbauten auf Capri. Leipzig (1900).

Maximilian Ihm: Die sogenannte « Villa Iouis » des Tiberius auf Capri und andere Suetoniana, in Hermes, Zeitschrift für Classische Philologie, 36, 1901.

Edwin Cerio: L'avvaloramento archeologico di Capri, in Le Pagine dell'Isola, Raccolta bibliografica di Capri, edita da Edwin Cerio. Napoli 1921.

Amedeo Maiuri: Grotte-ninfei imperiali nell'Isola di Capri, in Bollettino d'Arte, 25, 1931.

Paolino Mingazzini: Edizione Archeologica della Carta d'Italia al 100.000, Foglio 196, Vico Equense (Penisola Sorrentina ed Isola di Capri). Firenze 1931.

Paolino Mingazzini: Sul sito dell'Apragopoli menzionata da Suetonio, in Atti della R. Accademia di Archeologia, Lettere e Belle Arti di Napoli, Nuova Serie, 13, 1933-34.

Matteo Della Corte: Augustiana, *ibid.*

Matteo Della Corte: Capri, Apragopoli, Masgaba, *ibid.*

Amedeo Maiuri: Brevi note sulla vita di Augusto a Capri, *ibid.*

Amedeo Maiuri: Il Palazzo di Tiberio detto « Villa Jovis » a Capri, in Atti del 3° Congresso nazionale di Studi Romani, Roma 1934. Reprinted with the title Scavo di Villa Jovis a Capri, in the same author's Saggi di varia antichità. Venezia 1954.

D.M. Pippidi: Note sur une épigraphe funéraire grecque, métrique, de Capri, in Revista Clasica, 4-5, 1932-33, Bucaresti 1934.

Erik Wikén: Die Kunde der Hellenen von dem Lande und den Völkern der Apenninenhalbinsel bis 300 v. Chr. Lund 1937.

T.J. Dunbabin: The Western Greeks. Oxford 1948.

E.D. Phillips: Odysseus in Italy, in The Journal of Hellenic Studies, 73, 1953.

Filippo Magi: Un rilievo di Anacapri, in Rendiconti della Pontificia Accademia Romana di Archeologia, 28, 1954-55.

Paolino Mingazzini: Le grotte di Matermania e dell'Arsenale a Capri, in Archeologia Classica, 7, 1955.

Sven Hedenberg: Kejsar Tiberius, ett människoöde från antiken i psykiatrisk belysning. Stockholm 1956.

Amedeo Maiuri: Tacito e le ville di Tiberio a Capri, in Atene e Roma, Rassegna trimestrale dell'Associazione Italiana di Cultura Classica, Nuova Serie, 1, 1956.

Jean Bérard: La colonisation grecque de l'Italie méridionale et de la Sicile dans l'antiquité. L'historie et la légende. 2e éd., Paris 1957.

B.R. Motzo: Augusto in Capri, Masgaba, Apragopoli, in Annali delle Facoltà di Lettere Filosofia e Magistero dell'Università di Cagliari, 25, 1957.

Lord William Taylour: Mycenean Pottery in Italy and adjacent areas. Cambridge 1958.

Antonio Bellucci: Una iscrizione greco-romana a Capri, in the journal Fuidoro, 5, Napoli 1958.

Albert Esser: Cäsar und die Julisch-claudischen Kaiser im biologisch-ärztlichen Blickfeld, in Janus, Revue internationale de l'histoire des sciences de la médicine, de la pharmacie et de la technique, Suppléments, vol. I. Leiden 1958.

Alfonso De Franciscis: Le statue della Grotta Azzurra nell'isola di Capri. Capri 1964.

Humbert Kesel: ΚΑΠΡΙΗ ΝΗΣΟΣ ΙΤΑΛΙΑΣ. Antike Texte, Inschriften und Beiträge zur Geschichte der Insel Capri im Altertum. Typed manuscript, Dachau 1966 (1 ex. in Centro Caprense's library).

Lucia Vagnetti: I Micenei in Italia: la documentazione archeologita, in La Parola del Passato, 25, 1970.

John H. D'Arms: Romans on the Bay of Naples. A Social and Cultural Study of the Villas and Their Owners from 150 B.C. to A.D. 400. Loeb Classical Monographs, Harvard University Press, Cambridge, Massachusetts, 1970.

Giuseppe Salvia: Testimonianze letterarie ed epigrafiche su Capri antica. Tesi di Laurea in Letteratura Greca, Università degli Studi di Napoli, Facoltà di Lettere e di Filosofia, Anno Accademico 1970-1971. (1 ex. in Centro Caprense's library).

CAPRI IN THE MIDDLE AGES AND THE TIME OF THE SPANISH EMPIRE

Monumenta Germaniae Historica, Epistolarum Tomus I: Gregorii I Papae Registrum Epistolarum, Tomus I, Libri I-VII (Berlin 1891), no. I 52.

Philippus Ferrarius: Catalogus generalis Sanctorum, qui in Martyrologio Romano non sunt, etc. Venetiis 1625.

N. Squillante - T. Pagani: Vita della Venerabile Madre Suor Serafina di Dio, fondatrice di sette monasteri dell'Ordine Carmelitano. Incomminciata a descriversi dal P. Nicolò Squillante della Congregazione dell'Oratorio di Napoli, ma per la morte di questo proseguita e data alla luce dal P. Tomaso Pagani della medesima Congregazione. Napoli 1723.

M. Amari - C. Schiaparelli: L'Italia descritta nel « Libro del re Ruggero » compilato da Edrisi. Atti della R. Accademia dei Lincei, serie 2ª, vol. VIII, 1883.

Jean Le Fèvre: Journal de Jean Le Fèvre, evêque de Chartres, chancelier des Rois de Sicile Louis I et Louis II d'Anjou. Publié par H. Moranville, Paris 1887.

Diurnali del Duca di Monteleone, a cura di Michele Manfredi. Bologna 1895 and 1960.

Jean-Jacques Bouchard: Manuscript published in summary and excerpts by Lucien Marcheix, Un Parisien à Rome et à Naples en 1632, Paris s. a. (1897). For Chapter on Capri see Edwin Cerio, Capri nel Seicento (1934) and L'Ora di Capri (1950).

Bartolomeo Capasso: Le fonti della storia delle provincie napoletane dal 568 al 1500, con note del Dr. E. Oreste Mastrojanni. Napoli 1902.

Erich Caspar: Petrus Diaconus und die Montecassineser Fälschungen. Berlin 1909.

Adolf Hofmeister: Aus Capri und Amalfi, Der Sermo de virtute und Sermo de transitu S. Constantii und der Sarazenenzug von 991, in Münchner Museum, 1924, 4. Band, Heft 1-3.

Giobbe Ruocco: Sergio de Nicola e la Guerra del Vespro Siciliano. Sansevero 1925.

Salvatore Farace: Un gioiello d'arte ossia la chiesa di S. Michele Arcangelo detta Paradiso Terrestre, con un cenno della Ven. Madre Serafina di Dio e dei monumenti e ricordi di Anacapri. Napoli 1931.

Giobbe Ruocco: L'arte nel 300 a Capri. Il monumentale affresco del portale della chiesa della Certosa di S. Giacomo. Napoli 1932.

Edwin Cerio: Capri nel Seicento, documenti e note. Capri 1934.

Giobbe Ruocco: La identificazione di S. Costantino I Patriarca di Costantinopoli e Patrono di Capri attraverso alcuni codici latini, Appendice alla Rivista « Archivio Storico per la Provincia di Salerno », Anno II, N. 3-4. Napoli 1935.

Luigi Serra: La chiesa di S Costanzo a Capri, in Bollettino d'Arte, 30, 1936.

Giobbe Ruocco: Le incursioni vandalico-saracene e la conseguente autonomia comunale di Capri. Napoli 1947.

Giobbe Ruocco: La Basilica di S. Costanzo ossia il più vetusto monumento architettonico caprense religioso. Napoli 1948.

Giobbe Ruocco: Monumenta Longobarda et Latina ad historiam Caprehensiam pertinentia, a cura di Ettore Patrizi. Napoli 1948.

Giobbe Ruocc: Monumenta historica Caprehentia (saec. XIII). Napoli 1949.

Giobbe Ruocco: Capri nei suoi documenti archivistici (sec. XV-XVI-XVII). Napoli 1952.

Giobbe Ruocco: Capri nella sua storia e nei monumenti Angioini. Napoli 1953.

Giobbe Ruocco: Capri attraverso i suoi documenti del secolo XV nella storia del Regno di Napoli. Napoli 1955.

Giobbe Ruocco: Capri e Filippo IV di Spagna nel vicerealismo del Regno di Napoli attraverso i superstiti monumenti storici di Mons. Paolo Pellegrino alla seconda metà del secolo XVII. Napoli 1956.

Giobbe Ruocco: Capri attraverso i suoi documenti del secolo XVI nella storia del Regno di Napoli, Vol. I-II. Napoli 1955-1956.

Roberto Pane: Capri. Venezia 1954.

Roberto Pane: Capri — Mura e volte. Seconda edizione riveduta e ampliata. Napoli 1965.

Eugenio Aprea: Capri. La Certosa di S. Giacomo. Napoli 1969.

Anna Maria Pane: Le numerazioni dei fuochi di Capri e di Anacapri dal 1500 al 1700. Tesi di laurea in storia contemporanea. Università degli Studi di Napoli. Facoltà di Lettere e Filosofia. Anno accademico 1972-73. (1 ex. in Centro Caprense's library).

CAPRI UNDER THE BOURBONS

[Carl Joseph Stegmann:] Fragmente über Italien aus dem Tagebuch eines jungen Deutschen, I-II. Printed 1789 without information about author or place.

August Kopisch: Entdeckung der Blauen Grotte auf der Insel Capri, in the annual Italia, Berlin 1838. Also in the author's Gesammelte Werke, Berlin 1856.

Franz Dibelius: Zur Geschichte der Blauen Grotte auf Capri, in Neue Jahrbücher für das klassische Altertum, Geschichte und deutsche Literatur und Pedagogik, 33, Berlin 1914.

Mariano d'Ayala: Memorie storiche-militari dal 1734 al 1815. Napoli 1835.

Francesco Alberino: La presa di Capri. Poemetto con prefazione di Raffaello Flaminio. Napoli 1892.

E.M. Church: Sir Richard Church in Italy and Greece. London 1905.

Sir Lees Knowles: The British in Capri 1806-1808. London 1918.

Edwin Cerio: La letteratura sulla Presa di Capri, in Le Pagine dell'Isola, Aprile 1922.

Edwin Cerio: La presa di Capri cantata da un prete anacaprese, in the journal Fuidoro, 7-8, 1922.

Edwin Cerio: La presa di Capri in un frammento raro di MS, in Le Pagine dell'Isola, Capri s. a.

Sir Lees Knowles: The Taking of Capri. London 1923.

Pietro Colletta: Relazione della conquista di Capri, published by Nino Cortese, Lettere e scritti inediti di P. Colletta, in Archivio Storico delle Province Napoletane, Nuova Serie, Anno II, 1925.

Maurice Perrot: Deux Expéditions Insulaires Françaises: Surprise de Jersey en 1781, Prise de Capri en 1808. Paris 1929.

Piero Pieri - Ernesto Simion: La Presa di Capri (4-17 ottobre 1808), in Rivista di Cultura Marinara, fascicoli di maggio e di luglio-agosto, 1930.

Giobbe Ruocco: La scoperta della Grotta Azzurra nella storia di Capri — Angelo Ferraro. Napoli 1934.

Giobbe Ruocco: Capri nel movimento del Regno di Napoli al 1799. Napoli 1952.

Giobbe Ruocco: Capri nelle sue pagine di storia al 1806-1808. Napoli 1958.

Jürgen Schultze: Heinrich Fried und die Blaue Grotte von Capri, in Wallraf-Richartz-Jahrbuch, 35, Köln 1973.

CAPRI AFTER 1860

C.W. Allers: Capri. München s. a. (1892).

C.W. Allers: La Bella Napoli. Stuttgart 1893.

Johannes Proelss: Deutsch-Capri in Kunst, Dichtung, Leben. Historischer Rückblick und poetische Blütenlese. Oldenburg und Leipzig s. a. (1901).

Edwin Cerio: Capri attraverso la vita di Ignazio Cerio, volume primo: La vita e la figura di un uomo. Le Pagine dell'Isola (Roma 1921).

R.M. Dawkins: Norman Douglas. Rome—Milan—Naples 1952.

Kenneth Macpherson: Omnes eodem cogimur. Some notes written following the death of Norman Douglas 9 February 1952. Privately printed 1953.

Richard Aldington: Pinorman. Personal Recollections of Norman Douglas, Pino Orioli and Charles Prentice. London 1954.

Nancy Cunard: Grand Man. Memories of Norman Douglas. With extracts from his letters ... and a bibliographical note by Cecil Woolf. London 1954.

Cecil Woolf: A Bibliography of Norman Douglas. The Soho Bibliographies. London 1954.

Ian Greenlees: Norman Douglas. London 1957.
Lewis Leary: Norman Douglas. New York - London 1968.

AXEL MUNTHE AND THE VILLA SAN MICHELE

Knut Bonde: I skuggan av San Michele. Stockholm 1946.
Gustaf Munthe: Axel Munthe. Stockholm 1949.
Gustaf Munthe - G. Uexküll-Schwerin: Das Buch von Axel Munthe. München 1951.
Boken om Axel Munthe, Capri och San Michele, see under Literature with General and Mixed Contents.
Amedeo Maiuri: Ricordo di Axel Munthe, in Capri Segreta, la Rivista del Mezzogiorno Turistico, Anno VIII, Num. 37 (3), 15 maggio - 15 giugno 1962.
Hilding Thylander: Inscriptions latines de San Michele d'Axel Munthe, in Skrifter utgivna av Svenska Institutet i Rom, 4°, XXII = Opuscula Romana, IV. Lund 1962.
Josef Oliv: Axel Munthe, cosmopolita, medico, esteta e filantropo, in Symposium CIBA, Vol. 10, No. 3, 1962.
Arvid Andrén: Classical Antiquities of the Villa San Michele, in Skrifter utgivna av Svenska Institutet i Rom, 4°, XXIII = Opuscula Romana, V. Lund 1965.
Josef Oliv: Vägen till San Michele. Preface by Arvid Andrén. Stockholm 1972.
Staffan Tjerneld: Den mystiske dr Munthe. En biografi om herren till San Michele. Stockholm 1973.
Arvid Andrén: Mito e realtà nella Villa San Michele, in Studia Romana in honorem Petri Krarup septuagenarii. Odense 1976.

FOLKLORE

Gustav Floerke: Die Insel der Sirenen. Capresische Dorfgeschichten. Mit 25 Zeichnungen von Franz Arndt und Ch. Krohn. München 1879.

Gaetano Amalfi: Tiberio a Capri secondo la tradizione popolare. Trani 1893.

ADDENDA

Regarding the obscure plans and acts of Sejanus, reference can now be made to: Dieter Hennig: L. Aelius Seianus, Untersuchungen zur Regierung des Tiberius (Vestigia, Beiträge zur alten Geschichte, Band 21), München 1975.

An Impossible Woman. The Memories of Dottoressa Moor of Capri. Edited and with an Epilogue by Graham Greene. London 1975.

Mark Holloway: Norman Douglas. A Biography. London 1976.

Map of Capri and Illustrations

The numbers on the map indicate:

 1 Monte Tiberio
 2 Monte San Michele
 3 Monte Tuoro
 4 Castiglione with medieval castle
 5 Monte Solaro with medieval castle
 6 Monte Santa Maria
 7 Due Mari - Le Parate
 8 Marina Grande
 9 Marina Piccola
10 Scoglio delle Sirene
11 Scoglio dell'Unghia Marina
12 Faraglioni
13 Tragára
14 Punta Tragára
15 Porto di Tragára
16 Monacóne
17 Punta del Mónaco
18 Punta Trásete
19 Punta Campetiello
20 Punta del Pino
21 Punta Carena
22 Punta di Mulo
23 Villa Jovis
24 Pharus
25 Greek wall of Capri
26 Capri's piazza
27 Church of S. Salvatore
28 Church of S. Michele
29 Hotel Quisisana
30 Via Camerelle
31 Certosa
32 Parco Augusteo
33 Via Krupp
34 Palazzo Inglese
35 Cemeteries of Capri
36 Truglio
37 Campo Pisco

202

38 Contrada Torra	51 Cemetery of Anacapri	64 Torre della Guardia
39 Church of S. Costanzo	52 Church of S. Sofia	65 Mígliara
40 Hotel Grotta Azzurra	53 Church of S. Michele	66 Grotta Azzurra
41 Palazzo a Mare	54 Church of S. Maria	67 Grotta Rossa
42 Bagni di Tiberio	di Costantinopoli	68 Grotta Verde
43 Villa Fortino	55 Caprile	69 Grotta dell'Arco
44 Roman harbour	56 Ceselle	70 Grotta Castiglione
45 « Phoenician Steps »	57 Damecúta	71 Grotta Fra Felíce
46 Church of S. Antonio	58 Grádola	72 Grotta dell'Arsenale
47 Capodimonte	59 Veterino	73 Grotta Oscura
48 Villa San Michele	60 Timberino	74 Grotta dei Preti
49 Castello Barbarossa	61 Pozzo	75 Grotta di Matromania
50 Church of S. Maria	62 Orrico	76 Grotta Bianca
Cetrella	63 Torre Materita	77 Grotta Meravigliosa

Fig. 1.   Palaeolithic stone implement from the excavations near Hotel Quisisana. Polished axe of serpentine and painted clay vase from the Grotta delle Felci. Istituto Antropologico dell'Università di Napoli. Photo: Soprintendenza alle Antichità delle Province di Napoli e Caserta, Naples.

Fig. 2.   Incised pottery from the Grotta delle Felci. Istituto Antropologico dell'Università di Napoli. Photo: Soprintendenza alle Antichità delle Province di Napoli e Caserta, Naples.

Fig 3. Part of the Greek ring wall of the town of Capri. Photo: Soprintendenza alle Antichità delle Province di Napoli e Caserta, Naples.

Fig. 4. The « Phoenician Steps » leading up to the medieval gateway of Anacapri and the chapel of San Michele. Photo: Soprintendenza alle Antichità delle Province di Napoli e Caserta, Naples.

Fig. 5.   The precipice of Monte Tiberio, with the ruins of the Villa Jovis and the chapel of Santa Maria del Soccorso. Photo: Soprintendenza alle Antichità delle Province di Napoli e Caserta, Naples.

Fig. 6.   The main entrance to the Villa Jovis. Photo: Soprintendenza alle Antichità delle Province di Napoli e Caserta, Naples.

Fig. 7.   The south-west corner of the Villa Jovis, with the entrance, and in the background, Pharus, the ancient lighthouse. Photo: Soprintendenza alle Antichità delle Province di Napoli e Caserta, Naples.

Fig. 8.   One of the water cisterns of the Villa Jovis. Photo: Soprintendenza alle Antichità delle Province di Napoli e Caserta, Naples.

Fig. 9. Floor of variegated marble from the Villa Jovis, now in front of the high altar in the church of Santo Stefano. Photo: Soprintendenza alle Antichità delle Province di Napoli e Caserta, Naples.

Fig. 10.   Bronze statuette of an Egyptian pharaoh, found in 1922 on
the north slope of Castiglione. Owned by Donna Laetitia Cerio-Holt,
Capri. Photo: Ninuccio, Capri.

214

Fig. 11.   Marble statue of a toga-clad Roman, found near Truglio towards
the end of the 18th century. Formerly in the Vatican Museums, now in
Musée du Louvre, Paris. Photo Chuzeville, Paris.

Fig. 12. Marble portrait head of Augustus, found on the site of the Villa San Michele, now in the possession of Axel Munthe's heirs. Photo Vasari, Rome.

216

Fig. 13.   Marble portrait head of a Roman, found on Capri. British Museum. Photo British Museum.

217

Fig. 14. Marble bust of unknown origin, traditionally considered as a portrait of Tiberius, more probably recognized as one of Germanicus, the Emperor's nephew. Villa San Michele, Anacapri. Photo: Deutsches Archäologisches Institut, Rome.

218

Fig. 15.   Marble well head from the Villa Jovis. Museo Archeologico
Nazionale, Naples. Photo Anderson, Rome.

Fig. 16.   Marble well head from Capri. Formerly in the Palazzo Colombrano, Naples. British Museum. Photo British Museum.

Fig. 17.   Marble altar found at Pozzo, Anacapri. Formerly in the collection of Sir W. Hamilton, Naples. British Museum. Photo: British Museum.

221

Fig. 18.   Marble relief from the Villa Jovis. Museo Archeologico Nazionale, Naples. Photo Anderson, Rome.

Fig 19.   The Mithras relief from Capri. Museo Archeologico Nazionale,
Naples. Photo Alinari.

Fig. 20.   Marble torso of a youth, found in the Villa di Damecuta. Photo: Soprintendenza alle Antichità delle Province di Napoli e Caserta, Naples.

Fig. 2. Statue of a Triton, found in the Grotta Azzurra in 1964, as in presented itself to the photographer just after the rescue.

Fig. 22.   Statue of a Sea God, found in the Grotta Azzurra in 1975. Photo:
Soprintendenza alle Antichità delle Province di Napoli e Caserta, Naples.

Fig. 23. Castello Barbarossa, Anacapri. Photo Alinari.

Fig. 24.   The Byzantine interior of the church of San Costanzo, with columns partly taken from the ruins of a Roman villa. Photo Ninuccio, Capri.

228

Fig. 25.   The church of Sant'Anna, in Capri. Photo « Grafia », Rome.

Fig. 26.   The medieval Palazzo della Regina, now Palazzo Cerio, and the baroque Façade of the church of Santo Stefano. Photo « Grafia », Rome.

Fig. 27.   La Certosa di San Giacomo. The church and the campanile seen from the large cloister. Photo: Soprintendenza alle Antichità delle Province di Napoli e Caserta, Naples.

Fig. 28. The majolica floor representing the Garden of Eden, in the church of San Michele, Anacapri. Made in 1761 by L. Chiaiese, after a drawing by F. Solimena. Photo White, Capri.

Fig. 29. Painting by E. Fischetti, representing French troops landing on the west coast of Capri, October 4th, 1808. Museo della Certosa di San Martino, Naples. Photo Alinari.

Fig. 30.   Painting by E. Fischetti, representing Joachim Murat with officers at Massa during the attack against Capri, October 4th, 1808. Museo della Cartosa di San Martino, Naples. Photo Alinari.

234

INDEX

Dragut Rais 105
Due Mari 7, 124, 129
Duhn, Friedrich von 24
Dumas, Alexandre 138, 140, 150

Edrisi 94
Egizio, Matteo 38
Elephantis 56
Ercolano, Hotel 29
Esser, Albert 52
Etruria, Etruscans 17, 21
Ewers, Hans Heinz 141

Faráce, Antonio 134
Faraglioni, 46, 164
Féola, Giuseppe 46, 67 f., 72 f., 76 f., 84 f., 174, 179
Ferdinand IV (I) of Naples 65 f., 120 f., 122, 126, 128, 130 f.,
    135
Ferrarius, Philippus 92
Ferráro, Angelo 135, 140
Fersen, Jacques d'Adelswärd 160 f.
Fischetti, Odoardo 134
Flannigan, Lucy 159 f.
Fortino, see Villa Fortino
Fravicína 73
Frederick I Barbarossa 94, 137
Frederick II of Aragon 103
Frederick II of Hohenstaufen 94 f.
Friedländer, Immanuel 24, 26, 27
Fries, Ernst 135 f.
Furchheim, Friedrich 82, 137, 186
Fyodorovna, Maria 162

Gábrici, Ettore 23
Galli, Li 18, 20
Gallo, Bishop 72, 124

Hackert, Philip 140
Hádrawa, Norbert 65-67, 70, 74, 79, 84, 121, 126, 128-130,
    179
Haeckel, Ernst 144
Hagesandrus 81, 85
Hamill, John 132 f., 134
Hamilton, Sir William 66 f., 128, 130
Hamilton, Lady Emma 130
Haptmann, Gerhart 148
Hecataeus 26
Hedenberg, Sven 52
Herakleitos 19
Herculaneum 120 f.
Herodes Agrippa, see Agrippa, Marcus Julius
Hesiod 17, 18, 25
Hesychios 27 f.
Heyse, Paul 148
Hiddigeigei 144, 148, 184
Hiero I of Syrakousai 28, 33
Horace 15, 166
Hypatos 38 f., 141

Ihm, Maximilian 62
Ischia 21, 23-25, 29, 33
Isole Eólie, see Aeoliae
Isole dei Ciclópi 20

James, Henry 170
Jerome, Thomas Spencer 153 f., 168
Joan I of Anjou 97-100, 169
Joan II of Anjou 101
John, Bishop of Sorrento 90
Josephus, Flavius 50, 54-56, 59
Justinian 90
Juvenal 47